MONEY DOESN'T GROW ON TREES!

Paul Mason
Illustrated by Mike Gordon

WAYLAND

First published in 2010 by Wayland.

Copyright ©Wayland 2010

Wayland
338 Euston Road
London NW1 3BH

Wayland Australia
Level 17/207 Kent Street
Sydney NSW 2000

Editor: Nicola Edwards
Designer: www.rawshock.co.uk

British Library Cataloguing in Publication Data

Mason, Paul
    Money doesn't grow on trees:
    all about managing your money.
    1. Finance, Personal--Juvenile literature.
    I. Title II. Gordon, Mike.
    332'.024-dc22

ISBN: 978 0 7502 5899 9

Printed in China.

Wayland is a division of Hachette Children's Books,
an Hachette UK company.
www.hachette.co.uk

CONTENTS

Money all around!	4
How much money do we need?	6
Are you a spender or a saver?	8
Getting with a plan	12
Don't be a budget muppet	14
Smart savers …	16
…And savvy spenders	18
Becoming independent	20
Banks and money	22
Borrowing money	26
Credit cards: money munchers	30
Tempted to borrow	32
Growing your own money	34
Risks and rewards	36
Tax and inflation	40
The P word – Pensions	42
Test your money skills	44
Glossary	46
Further information	47
Index	48

MONEY ALL AROUND!

If you want to catch a bus, buy a drink, go to the cinema, or do a thousand other ordinary things, what do you need? Money! Money is all around us, all the time. We use money so often that most of us take it for granted (at least until we run out). But is money as simple as it seems?

Using banknotes instead of chickens or pigs when you wanted to buy something made life a lot easier!

Why was money invented?

Money was invented to make the world an easier place to live in. Before money, people used to exchange goods to get things they needed. They might swap a chicken for some vegetables, for example. For this to work, they had to find someone who had some spare vegetables, and who wanted a chicken.

As soon as money appeared, life became much easier. You could sell your chicken for money, and use the money to buy some vegetables. It was much less bother than the old way! You might even have a bit left over, to save for next week's vegetables.

Early money

It took quite a long time before everyone agreed what money should look like. In China, they used bits of silver as money. On Pacific islands, people used cowrie shells. In New Guinea, it was pigs – try putting one of those in your back pocket when you nip to the shops!

Money today

Today, cash money takes the form of banknotes and coins. Originally these were worth something: a British pound note, for example, could be taken to the Bank of England and swapped for 1lb (450g) of gold. Today, though, banknotes and coins are only valuable because we agree they are.

MONEY MATTERS

    ¥ $ £ € %

Money worries

Students worry more about their debts than anything else. **59%** say debt is their biggest worry, just **29%** worry about their studies, and **12%** about their social lives.

Money in the bank

Unlike in the olden days, most people no longer keep their money in a box under the bed. Instead, it's usually kept in a bank or savings account. People never get to see all their money together. Instead they get a statement: a printout showing how much money is in each of their accounts.

Confused by money? This book will soon turn on the lightbulb of understanding!

Managing your money

Managing your money is one of the key skills of modern life. NOT managing your money is a bit like carrying around a bucket of water with holes in it: your money leaks away, bit by bit. However much more you pour in, the bucket never quite gets filled up. Leaking money in this way makes life tougher: shopping expeditions, going to see a live band, and holidays, for example, all become hard to afford.

Fortunately, it's not that tricky to manage your money well. This book is full of tips to help you make sure that as much of your money as possible remains yours – instead of dribbling away!

"MONEY'S DULL." Duh! The only time money's dull is when you don't have enough.

HOW MUCH MONEY DO WE NEED?

We all need money — without it, living in the modern world would be impossible. Today, only a tiny number of people could build a home, make clothes, or feed themselves without money. Most of us lack the skills that would be needed. But how much money do we need?

What you need – and what you want

One way to think of your money needs is as a pyramid. The bottom layer is made up of the things you really *need* to survive. The top of the pyramid is made up of things you definitely don't need, but do *want*. Everything else comes somewhere in between.

Things you really don't need (but might like)

Luxuries such as a new TV (even though the old one isn't actually broken) belong here.

Luxury extras

Things that are a good idea

Holidays, TVs, computer games, a second winter coat, gym membership – these are all things that many people enjoy, but they aren't crucial.

Things that make life more comfortable

Most people think it is a good idea to have some savings. That way, if your new bicycle is stolen, your sofa catches fire, or some other unforeseen expense comes up, it won't be a problem.

Things you need to survive

Once they have enough money to survive, people usually try to make life a bit better. They might buy more clothes or a bicycle, or donate money to charity, for example.

We all need money to pay for food, clothes, and somewhere to live: without these, it would be impossible for most of us to survive.

The enough-money line

Could you put a ruler across the pyramid to say where a this-is-enough-money line should go? Almost everyone draws the line in a slightly different place. For some people, a simple home and a few possessions are enough. Others feel it is important to own the latest gadgets, a fast car and a big house.

One thing is for sure: the higher up the pyramid you put the line, the more money you will need. Or you can think of it another way: the less money you have, the lower down the pyramid the line HAS to go.

Some people desire nice cars, fancy clothes and the latest mobiles that draw attention to themselves — but lots of others manage happily without them.

MONEY MATTERS

¥ $ £   €   %

"I need more money – my friends can buy more stuff than me."
Don't worry about keeping up with your friends – worry about the things YOU want. If you can't afford them now, turn to page 13 for ideas on how to get the money together.

What money can do for you – and what it can't

There's no doubt that money is very useful stuff – but it can't do everything! These are just a few of the things money can and can't do for you:

Money can:	Money can't:
• Make you feel secure, knowing that even if things go wrong, you will have somewhere to live and food on the table • Make life more comfortable and easier • Get you noticed (maybe because you drive a fancy car, or maybe because you give a lot to charity)	• Make you fit and healthy • Bring you good friends, or love • Make you feel happy or sad if you aren't already

Which are you – spender or saver?

This quiz will help you work out if you're a spender or a saver, or somewhere in between. It's important to be honest with your answers! You'll find it easy to work out what the answers 'should' be, if you want to come out as a spender or saver – but what's the point of that?

Striking a balance between spending and saving is the best way to avoid money problems.

1) In your bedroom

Have a look around your bedroom. Which toys or gadgets have you bought (or persuaded someone to buy for you) in the last year? If so, how many times have you used them, on average?
a) Fewer than 10 times
b) Between 10 and 25 times
c) Over 25 times

2) In your wardrobe

Now try the same trick with your wardrobe: look at the new pairs of shoes or items of clothing that have arrived there in the last year (you can leave out school uniform). Work out on average how many times they have been worn:
a) Fewer than 5 times
b) Between 5 and 20 times
c) More than 20 times

3) Stashing your cash

When you're going out for the day with your friends, do you:

a) Automatically take plenty of money with you, because you might see something you want to buy?

b) Take a little bit of money, to buy a drink or some food?

c) Just take enough for the bus fare home: if you need more, you can always come and get it!

4) At the shops

Imagine you're at the shops with your friends. Your best friend buys a new pair of boots, and they look really good. Do you:

a) Buy a pair just like them, right there and then?

b) Decide to think about it, and come back next weekend to see if you still like them?

c) Congratulate your friend on such a good buy (while secretly thinking they were a bit of a waste of money...)?

5) At the end of the week

It's the end of the week, six days since you last got your allowance. What are you thinking?

a) "Oh no – there's none left. And I still haven't paid Tom back from last week. Eek!"

b) "I think I can hear a bit of change jingling in my pocket – but only a bit!"

c) "Nice to see my savings account going up a little bit more this week. Just another £37,862.29 to go until I can afford that Porsche. And the driving lessons, of course..."

Oh dear — no money, no pizza (and no DVDs, new jeans, concert tickets, etc, etc.).

How did you do?

Tot up your answers, and see whether you had mostly a), b) or c).

Mostly a):

You're definitely a spender! Your allowance probably never lasts the week. It would be a good idea to try to stop yourself making impulse buys. Maybe you could decide always to wait a week before buying something you've seen and want?

Mostly b):

Like most people, you're sometimes a spender, and sometimes a saver. You probably always have a bit of money, but not enough to buy something big. It's important that you recognize when it's a good idea to spend money, and when it's better to keep hold of it.

Mostly c):

There's no doubt you're a saver. You're careful about what you spend your money on, and you probably have plenty set aside. Remember, though – it's OK to spend money on things you really want, as long as you can afford them!

GETTING WITH A PLAN

The world is brimful of things to do, and stuff to spend
your money on. A new games console, the latest clothes, a
skateboard, tickets for the ballet, your favourite football
team's kit, presents for your friends, gifts to charities — the
list is almost endless! But no one has the time or money to do
everything, so how do you decide what you're going to use
your money for? The answer is to make a plan!

Dreaming of crucial new stuff?
Make a money plan!

Money plan, stage 1:
What do you want?

The first step towards making a money
plan is to decide on what you want to
use your money for. A simple example
would be if you want to get a new guitar,
one that costs £99.99. Making a money
plan will help you work out how you
can afford it.

Money plan, stage 2:
What do you already have?

The next step is to work out what you
already have that can be put towards
buying the guitar. Maybe you have
£75.00 in a savings account, for example
You probably won't want to put all of
it towards a guitar – what if tickets for
your favourite band come up for sale?
But you could decide that a third of your
savings can be put towards the guitar.

Money plan, stage 3:
Planning for your goals

You have £25.00 from your savings
account, but the guitar costs £100.00. So
there's £75.00 to go – where is it going
to come from? The next stage of your
money plan is to make a list of the
places you can get more money to put
towards your goals:

Selling off old stuff can be a great way to make a bit of cash. Just make sure you don't get carried away and sell everything off cheap.

• Allowance

If you get regular allowance, say £5.00 a week, you might decide to save half of it towards the guitar. That's £10.83 per month. (Every third month has five weeks in it, not four. To work out a monthly income, multiply the weekly amount by 13 [4 weeks + 4 weeks + 5 weeks = 13], then divide the answer by 3.)

• Selling stuff

Perhaps you have some things you could sell? Maybe you could get your Mum or Dad to help you sell your old stuff at a car-boot sale. Old toys, computer games you don't play any more, or books that are too young for you could all earn a bit of money towards the guitar.

• Earn some money

Do you have, or could you get, a job? It might not be an 'official' job, like working in a shop. Maybe you could invest in some buckets, sponges and carwash liquid, and start a car-washing business in your street?

Money plan, stage 4: Kerrang!

Once you know how much money is coming in, you can easily work out when you'll be able to afford the guitar:

Savings	£25
Selling old stuff	£14
Allowance	£10.83 a month (2 months = £21.66)
Carwash business	£26 a month (2 months = £52)

Total in 2 months =   £112.66

So inside 2 months, you'll be able to buy yourself the guitar!

DON'T BE A BUDGET MUPPET

Some people drift through life without ever really worrying about money. They spend whatever they like, and don't think too much about how to pay for it. This is **OK** if you're the heiress to a million-dollar fortune. For ordinary people, though, it is a dangerous way of thinking, because it can lead you into debt. Fortunately, there's an easy way to avoid this. It's called a budget.

Income and outgoings

The first step in making yourself a budget is to work out your *income*. Income is the money that comes in, as allowance or earnings. Maybe you get £5.00 a week allowance, and £6.00 a week from your car-wash business. Your income is £11.00 a week, or £47.67 a month.

Next, you need to make a list of your *outgoings*. Outgoings are the things you spend money on. The list might look something like this:

If there's not enough coming in, maybe it's time to think of ways of earning a bit more cash?

Cinema tickets:	£11 per month (2 visits)
Clothes:	£15 per month (average)
Bus fare to meet friends:	£8 per month
Bike equipment:	£10 per month (average)
Sweets, drinks, etc:	£8 per month
Total:	**£52 per month**

If this is what your income and outgoings look like, you're in trouble! There's £47.67 coming in each month – and £52 going out. Not only are you not saving any money, you have a *deficit* of £4.33.

Balancing the budget

When outgoings are more than income, your budget is *unbalanced*. There are only two ways to balance it:
1) Increase your income
2) Decrease your outgoings

In the example above, the only way to increase your income would be to wash more cars. But there are plenty of ways to decrease your outgoings:
• Only go to the cinema once a month
• Buy fewer clothes
• Walk or cycle to meet your friends
• Spend less on your bike
• Kick the sweetie habit

Which of these you choose depends on what's important to you. If you love films, and live a short walk from town, you might give up the bus rides. The important thing is to pick which thing you'll give up – and stick to your decision.

If things go really well, maybe you'll be able to give your friends jobs too. Maybe you'll have to!

MONEY MATTERS

Money matters: budget tips
Here are some ideas for saving money and making your outgoings smaller:
• Make your own sandwiches instead of buying lunch or snacks
• Go for a run (free!) instead of going to the pool (costs money)
• Walk or cycle instead of catching the bus
• Get old clothes altered, instead of buying new ones

"Don't worry about whether you can afford it now – it'll be OK, we'll sort it out later"
Er – how will it magically get sorted out later? If *you* don't worry about it, who will?

SMART SAVERS ...

One of the reasons for needing to balance your budget (see pages 14 and 15) is so that you don't get into debt. In fact, it is a good idea to try to make your outgoings less than your income, so that there is a bit of money left over each month. That way, you can build up some savings.

Why bother with savings?

There are two main reasons to build up some savings: to make a big purchase, and in case of an unforeseen (and expensive) disaster.

• Buying something big

If you get in the habit of saving, you will have money set aside to pay for big purchases such as a new scooter, mobile phone, etc.

• Unforeseen events

Imagine if, when you are older, your washing machine or TV breaks, or you lose your job. If you have some money saved up, unexpected events like these don't have to be a disaster. You can use your savings to put things right.

Saving is a skill

Some people are better at saving than others. If you have done the quiz on pages 10 and 11, you'll have a good idea of whether you're a saver or spender. If you came out as being a spender, saving money is a skill you will need to work at. The good news is, saving doesn't have to be painful. The 'Money matters' features will give you some ideas of how to start.

If disaster strikes, it's good to have a bit of money put aside to make things right again.

Become a 10% saver

One of the best ways to save money is to decide that you will put 10% of all your income into a savings account. You will not miss the money, and your savings will quickly build up.

Savings accounts

Most people keep their savings in a savings account. You can open one of these at banks, building societies, or the post office. When you open it, you get a unique account number for paying in and taking out money. You will be sent regular statements, showing how much money is in your account. These usually come either once a month or every three months.

Give up one thing

Increase your savings by giving up one thing, and putting the money into your savings account instead. You could give up shop-bought sandwiches, canned drinks, chocolate, renting DVDs – almost anything that costs money.

Types of savings account

There are two main types of savings account:

• No-notice accounts

These are accounts where you can take your money out again without warning the bank.

• Notice accounts

With a notice account, you have provide warning (or 'notice') that you want to take the money out.

While your money is being kept by the bank or building society, they pay you a small amount each month for letting them have it. This is called *interest* (see page 26 for more information). You usually get more interest on a notice account than a no-notice account.

You may think it's safely hidden — but really a savings account might be a better place to put your cash.

... AND SAVVY SPENDERS

Even when you are spending money, it's possible to save — by spending less than normal on the things you buy. It does not take much research to find the best prices for the things you need. Lots of people call this getting "good value for money". But is low price the only thing that makes a purchase good value?

What is 'good value'?

Just because something is cheap, that doesn't necessarily mean it is good value. Here are some of the other things you might want to think about when deciding if something is worth buying:

• Will it last a long time?

Is the thing you want to buy well made? A bike that lasts five years is better value than one that falls apart after six months – even if it costs three times as much.

• How long will you want it for?

A pair of purple velvet flares might seem like a good idea now, especially if they are cheap in a sale. But if next month you're embarrassed to wear them, they weren't a good buy.

• Are you paying for the label?

Sometimes you can buy almost the exact-same thing for far less money, but without a fashionable label on it. If it bothers you, just cut the 'unfashionable' labels out when you get home!

Discount vouchers

One way to save money on your shopping is to keep an eye open for discount vouchers. You find these in all kinds of places: on the Internet,

They might be cheap, but that REALLY doesn't mean they're a good idea...

in newspapers, on the packaging for products, even put through your door with free newspapers. (Hint: if your parents don't collect these for things they usually buy, keep them ready for when you go shopping. If you helpfully hand them over at the checkout, maybe you'll get a reward!)

"I got this in the sale – it was half price, so I've saved £15!"
You have – but only if it was something you wanted anyway. If you didn't really need it, you've *spent* £15, not saved it!

Looking for the SALE sign

Sales can be a great place to pick up good value products. You might be able to get jeans or trainers for half price, or even less. The trouble is, it's easy to get carried away and buy things just because they are cheap. But as long as you're buying something you already knew you needed, the SALE sign can point the way to good value.

Shopping around

It usually pays to compare different shops' prices, to find who sells the things you need cheapest. (Remember that Internet sites and catalogues usually charge postage, and if you have to send things back for a different size or colour that may cost money too.)

The 'shopping around' attitude isn't just for things like trainers and DVDs. When you're older, you will be able to apply it to savings and bank accounts, energy supplies, and just about anything else.

MONEY MATTERS

¥ $ £   €   %

Handy hints for spending less
- Never buy anything just because it's cheap
- Only buy things you really want
- Never spend money on the spur of the moment.

Sales can be good ways to save money — as long as you buy something you already wanted.

BECOMING INDEPENDENT

In most countries, before you are 18 your parents are partly responsible for your finances. Once you are 18, though, you are usually expected to manage your own money. This is also when many young people get their first job, or study away from home for the first time. So what's involved in managing your own money?

Opening a bank account

If you don't already have one, the first thing you will need to do is open a bank account. This is where any money you are paid will go, and is used to pay your costs. There's advice on what to look for in a bank account and how they work on pages 24 to 25.

"I have a student loan – that must be enough money for everything I need." Whether it's enough or not depends on what you spend. Make a budget to be sure that your money will go far enough to last until the end of term.

Income

When you start work or become a student, you will probably have more money coming in than ever before – whoppee! Don't forget, though: you also have a lot of new outgoings. Some of these are things you will have no choice but to pay, and are called *fixed costs*. Now the budgeting skills you developed in the past (see pages 14 to 15) are really going to come in handy.

When you first start managing your own money, it's very exciting, and can seem like a lot! It soon starts going out again too, though...

Setting a budget

The principles of setting yourself a budget are always the same: your income has to be the same as or more than your outgoings. It's useful to divide your outgoings into two categories: fixed costs (things you have to pay), and variable costs (things you can choose not to pay).

Fixed costs

Fixed costs start with the things at the bottom of the money-needs pyramid on page 6: food, shelter and clothing. You may also now have other fixed costs. If you are a student or training while working, maybe you have to buy paper, pens, books, and other study materials.

When making your budget, start with the fixed costs. The list might look like this:

Accommodation:	£200 per month
Food and drink:	£160 per month
Travel:	£40 per month
Study materials:	£40 per month
Gas and electricity*:	£25 per month
Total:	**£465 per month**

*Don't forget, if you are sharing a house with other people, costs like gas and electricity will be shared.

Variable costs

Variable costs are the things you can choose whether to spend money on. These come from nearer the top of the money-needs pyramid on page 6. They might include guitar lessons, long journeys to visit friends or family, holidays, or sports equipment.

Balancing the budget

Having listed all your outgoings, compare them to your income. It might look like this:

Fixed costs:	£465 per month
Variable costs:	£95 per month
Total:	**£560 per month**

If you have more than £560 per month of income, this is fine. If you have less, you have either to cut your variable costs, or find some way to increase your income.

A bit of sweating in a kitchen might earn you some sweating on the beach!

BANKS AND MONEY

Most of us think of money as cash — notes and coins with which we can buy things. But very few people actually keep all their money in this form. Most of our money is kept in banks. This means our money is kept secure, and makes getting cash or paying bills easy. But unless you manage your bank account carefully, it could be expensive to run.

Banks, in general, are very good at keeping your money safely.

A brief history of banking

The first banks were simply secure places to keep your money and valuables. For doing this, the bankers charged a fee, a bit like a storage charge, which was one of the ways they made money.

Next, banks started to offer their customers a service called a 'note of *credit*'. Instead of buying things with real money, you could hand over your note of credit for, say, a hundred pounds. The seller then took the note of credit to the bank, and was given the hundred pounds. Notes of credit made it possible to do business far away, in places where it would be risky to travel with real money. Of course, the bank charged for issuing notes of credit, so it made a bit of money on each one.

The bankers also realized that they didn't need to have all the money sitting in their bank all the time. They could lend some of it to other people, for which they also charged a fee, like a kind of rental charge on the money. This made them a bit more money.

MONEY MATTERS

¥ $ £ € %

Opening a bank account

Rules for opening a bank account depend on the bank and country. In some countries you have to be 18; in others, you can do it at 16. In most places, though, some sort of account is available to young people of 12 years old or more.

If you are able to open an account, you will need to show some official I.D., such as a passport and birth certificate, and prove your address. If you are under 18, one of your parents may have to come along with you, too.

Banking today

Today's banks work in a very similar way to the first banks. People put their money into the bank for safekeeping. The chance of everyone wanting to take out all their money at the same time is tiny, so the bank is able to *invest* some of it, to make more money.

One big difference from the past is that there are lots of new ways to take your money out of the bank (see 'Withdrawals' on page 24). Also, few banks still charge you for storing your money.

Current accounts

Most people keep their everyday money in a type of bank account called a *current account*. This is an account that is designed to allow you to pay in and withdraw money easily. It is not designed for keeping your savings in: for that you need to choose a different type of account (see pages 36 to 39 for more information).

Banks are always keen to sign up new customers, so it's worth shopping around to see who will give you the best welcome.

How bank accounts work

Once people have opened a current account, they use it to manage their day-to-day spending. The money they earn is paid in, and the money they spend goes out.

Withdrawals

There are lots of ways to withdraw money or pay bills using your current account, including:

• Use a cash card and *PIN number* to take money out at the cash-point machine.
• Use a debit card and PIN number to make payments.
• Write a cheque, which usually has to be guaranteed with a cheque-guarantee card (often your debit card is also a cheque-guarantee card).
• Transfer money using the Internet, if you have Internet access to your current account.

Paying bills

Many people pay their bills for costs such as accommodation, telephone or heating by cheque. Regular costs such as these can also be paid by standing order or direct debit:

• Standing orders are regular payments of an agreed amount of money. For example, if your rent is £250 per month, you might set up a standing order for £250 per month to your landlord's account. The bank then pays that each month until you tell it not to.
• Direct debits are an agreement to let money be taken from your account for a specific purpose. For example, your phone bill is probably different each month, so it cannot be paid with a standing order. A direct debit allows the phone company to take different amounts each time.

It's important to keep track of the money you pay in to and take out of your bank account.

Paying in

Soon after you open a bank account, the bank sends you a *paying-in book*. To pay in cash or cheques, you visit a branch of the bank, and hand in the money and the filled-in paying-in slip. The cashier tears out the filled-in page, and stamps it and the stub of the torn-out page to prove you have paid the money in.

You might only have overspent by a tiny bit, but the bank could still add surprisingly BIG charges as a result.

Money can also be paid in by computer transfer from another bank. Most large amounts of money, for example wages or student loans, are paid in this way.

The cost of banking

Most banks do not charge you for having a bank account, as long as you have some money. Sometimes, though, a person's bank account goes *overdrawn*. This means he or she has spent more than is in their account, so they owe the bank money. Banks usually charge their customer if this happens.

Some banks charge for sending statements, using cheques and other services. It pays to check what charges a bank could make before you open an account with them.

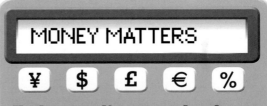

MONEY MATTERS

¥ $ £ € %

Understanding your bank statement

Bank statements usually have six pieces of information for each entry:

Date	Description	Details	Money out	Money in	Balance
This tells you the date of the transaction.	This tells you whether money came in/out, and who from/to.	Here you see if it was a cheque, card payment, direct debit, etc.	Sometimes called *debit*, this shows how much money went out.	Sometimes called *credit*, this shows how much money came in.	This tells you how much money was left after the payment in or out.

BORROWING MONEY

Sometimes even people who manage their money carefully find that they don't have enough. Maybe there has been a disaster such as a crashed car that has to be repaired. Or maybe the money is needed to start a business or buy a house, and the cost is too large an amount to save up. In cases like this, many people decide to borrow the money. Borrowing money is often called getting (or taking out) a loan.

How loans work

Loans can come from a variety of places. The most likely place for young people to get loans is from their friends (for small amounts) or their parents (for bigger amounts). Older people can also get loans from banks, building societies, and specialist loan companies.

Usually loans have to be paid back with regular payments over a specific time, for example every month for a year. This is called the *term* of the loan.

Interest

When you borrow money from your friends or parents, you usually only have to pay back the same amount as you borrowed. If you borrow money elsewhere, though, you usually have to pay back a little bit extra. This extra payment is caused *interest*. Charging interest is how banks and other financial organizations make money from loans. Interest is worked out as a percentage of the amount you borrowed. This figure is called the *interest rate*.

MONEY MATTERS

¥ $ £   €   %

Loans v. savings

As well as charging interest on loans, most banks pay interest on your savings. The interest rate charged on loans is always higher than the interest rate paid on savings.

Because you pay more interest on a loan than you earn on savings, it's almost always better to spend your savings than to take out a loan.

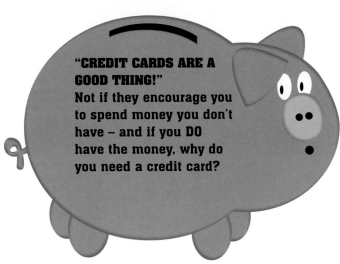

"CREDIT CARDS ARE A GOOD THING!"
Not if they encourage you to spend money you don't have – and if you DO have the money, why do you need a credit card?

Each statement lists the amount carried over, this month's spending, and the amount you owe. Unless you owe nothing, there will also be a note saying, 'Minimum payment', and an amount. This is the minimum you have to pay back that month.

The minimum payment trap

Paying off the minimum payment amount on a credit card won't pay off your debt. All it does is give the credit-card company some of your money. The debt still sits there, getting bigger, until your next statement. If all you do is pay off the minimum payment next time, the debt will carry on getting bigger, and bigger, and bigger – and each month, the card company is getting a bit of your money.

Pretty soon, you might find yourself in a situation where all you can afford to pay IS the minimum payment. That's when you're really trapped!

People who fall into the minimum payment trap soon find themselves dreading the day on which their credit-card bill arrives.

MONEY MATTERS

Credit v. debit cards

Credit cards are not the same as debit cards. A debit card is part of your current account. If you spend money on a debit card, the money is taken straight from your current account. Credit cards are separate from your current account, and have their own rules.

31

TEMPTED TO BORROW

Banks, credit card companies and other financial organizations are keen to lend money, because it's how they make profits. They make borrowing seem as easy and attractive as possible. But just because a loan is good for them, doesn't mean it's good for you. It pays to be aware of some of the language used to get you to borrow money.

Tricks of the (lending) trade

These are some of the ways in which banks, credit-card companies, shops, garages, and other organizations try to attract customers:

Offer: *'Buy now, pay later'*
These are offers where you get to take the goods away immediately, but don't have to pay for them for a long time – often six months or a year later. Sometimes they are advertised as, 'No interest' or, 'Interest free' for a set period of time.

Often found in: Shops selling furniture, electronic goods, and white goods (e.g. washing machines).
Danger: If you do not pay back the whole amount on time, you may be charged interest at a high rate. The interest may be **backdated**, starting from the moment you got the goods.

Offer: *'£100s cashback'*
These are offers where you get some cash back if you buy something or take out a loan. For example, you buy a camera for £350.00 and get £40.00 cashback.
Often found in: Cashback offers are everywhere.
Danger: If someone is offering you cashback, they must be making the cash from the deal in some other way. Probably, either you are paying too much for the goods, or paying too much interest on the loan.

MONEY MATTERS

¥ $ £   €   %

Making you feel special
Lenders try to make borrowers feel special and important. They say things like, 'You have been specially selected', or tell you about an, 'exclusive offer' available only to selected customers'. Language like this might make you feel happier about taking out the loan – but it won't help you to repay it!

BE A TOP DOG!

Offer: *Reward schemes*
These are schemes where you are rewarded every time you spend or borrow money. The reward is often in the form of points, which you can 'spend' on products selected by the company.

Often found in: Everywhere, but especially shops and credit-card companies.

Danger: As with cashback, the money for the rewards you are getting has to come from somewhere. The other danger is that you may be tempted to buy a different product from the one you really want, just for the reward.

'Loans are a good idea. After all, they are a way to buy what you want now, and pay for it later! Great!'
Not necessarily. When you take out a loan, you are actually agreeing to pay the lender part of your future income for months or years to come. So you won't be able to enjoy that money later on – which isn't great at all.

It's amazing what people will tell you when they want your money!

GROWING YOUR OWN MONEY

Most people earn money by having a job. But working is not the only way to make money. Once you have some money put aside, you can use it to make more. Using your money to try to make more money is called investing it. Investing is a bit like planting seeds: you plant your money somewhere, and wait for it to grow.

Plant your money in the right place, look after it carefully, and hopefully it will pay you back.

A capital idea

Capital is the name for something – for example, money, property or land – that you can use to earn money. (Income is the name for the money you earn.) When deciding how to invest your money, it is a good idea to keep your capital intact, and only risk changes in your income.

To understand why, imagine a fruit tree. Think of your capital as the tree itself, and the income as the fruit. If you start cutting branches off the tree (i.e. reducing your capital), you will end up getting less fruit next year (i.e. less income).

Making your capital work

Most people use their capital to make money by putting it into a savings account, where it will earn interest. The interest payments are their income. But there are other ways to invest your money:

• Investing in a business

For example, you and your friends might want to start up a business doing bike repairs, or clothes alterations. You would need tools or sewing kit, which cost money. You (or your Mum or Dad) might decide to buy these in return for a share of whatever money the business makes. Be sure it is clear how the investors will get their money out when they want it, though!

• Buying stocks and shares

Stocks and *shares* are a way of investing in big businesses. If you think next year lots of people will be buying bicycles, for example, you might decide to buy shares in a company that makes great bikes.

MONEY MATTERS

¥ $ £   €   %

Is money ever bad?
Your money has power. Whether you spend it, let a bank look after it, or invest it yourself, it can be used in various ways.

• Some accounts and investments might use your money to pay for manufacturing weapons, slave labour, and polluting industries, for example. These may be profitable, but some people would prefer that their money wasn't used in this way.

• Other accounts and investments make promises about how your money will be used. They may invest in renewable technology, organic farming, or fair-trade industries, for example. Some people prefer to know their money is being used in this way.

Earning money doesn't have to be dull or boring! Maybe you're good at making people laugh, or clowning around, and someone will pay you to do it.

RISKS AND REWARDS

People who want to invest their money have to ask themselves one very important question: 'How much risk am I willing to take?' The answer to this question depends on whether you can afford to lose some or all of the money. It also decides how much of a reward you could get for your investment.

A day at the races

Investing money is a bit like betting on a horse race. Imagine you're at the racetrack, and there's a horse that is almost certain to win. There are only two other horses in the race, one of them fat and the other old. Placing a bet on the young, slim horse is not likely to win you much money. In the investment world, near-certain winners like this are called a *safe* or *low-risk investment*.

The other extreme is to bet on the fat horse, or maybe the old one. No one expects either to cross the line first.

Betting on one of these could win you a lot of money! But there's also a big risk that you will *lose* everything. This is a *high-risk investment*.

Low risk, low reward

If you were down to your last pound coin, you probably wouldn't bet it on the fat horse or the old one. You'd rather be almost certain of winning a small amount than risk having nothing left. Investments work in the same way: if you cannot afford to lose your money, you need a safe or low-risk investment.

Regardless of which horse wins this race, you wouldn't bet on any of them unless you didn't mind losing your money.

High risk, high reward?

Now imagine you have £7.00 in your pocket, and you get your allowance tomorrow. You might feel willing to risk a pound on one of the high-risk horses. It won't really matter if you lose. Investing works the same way: if you can afford to lose some or all your money, you *could* choose a high-risk investment.

Making the right investment can be like backing a winning horse - but investing money, like gambling, is a risky business.

MONEY MATTERS

¥ $ £   €   %

Deciding on an investment

Once you have decided on the level of risk you are willing to take, and what kind of investment you need, these are some other things to consider:

- **How do I get my money out?**
  With some investments you have to give warning that you want your money back. Some savings accounts, for example, work in this way. You might have to let them know a month, three months or even a year in advance. It might be impossible to get your money back sooner, or you may *forfeit* some or all of the interest you would have earned.

- **How long can I leave the money there?**
  The value of many investments goes up and down. Imagine you have bought shares in a company, or a piece of Banksy artwork. In six months' time, they might be worth less than you paid for them. If you *had* to sell in six months, you would lose out. If you could afford to wait until prices rose again, it might still turn out to have been a good investment.

"I've found an investment that guarantees an unbelievable profit really quickly. I'm going to invest." If it seems too good to be true, it usually is. Read the small print of the deal very carefully: big profits almost never come with cast-iron guarantees.

37

Diversification

Diversification is the name for spreading your investments around. Investing your money in several different places makes it less likely that you could lose some or all of it. If all your money were invested in one place, it would be disastrous if that investment crashed in value. But if you split your money between four investments, one of them crashing is less serious.

A balanced portfolio

A group of investments is sometimes called a *portfolio*. Most investors aim to have a balanced portfolio. This means that they have a variety of investments, of different types and levels of risk. Imagine dividing your money in four:

• Quarter could go into a nice, safe savings account where you can get at it straight away

• Quarter could go into a long-notice savings account, which pays a higher rate of interest

• Quarter could be invested in shares

• Quarter could be spent on a piece of Banksy artwork, a rare vinyl album, or something else you think might increase in value

A portfolio like this would have a good balance between security and risk.

Some people choose to invest their money in art, or other objects they are interested in.

Money matters: judging your investment

How do you decide what kind of investment to make? Start by judging whether you can afford to lose some or all of your capital (the money you invest). The chart opposite will then help you decide where you could put your money:

Investment:	Typical risk:	Possible reward:	Investment level:
Savings account	Almost none: even if the bank fails, most governments guarantee to refund your savings.	Relatively low interest rates.	One of the safest places to put your money: up to 100% of it could go into savings accounts.
Stocks and shares	Because any business can fail, it is possible you could lose some, or even all, of your money.	The value of your shares *could* rise dramatically. You may also be paid a *dividend* if the company makes enough money.	Because the risk is higher, it would be unwise to invest more than you can afford to lose.
Investment funds	Investment funds buy shares in a variety of companies, so even if one goes bust, the others will still be there. This spreads the risk.	With less risk comes less reward. Also, the fund's managers will expect to be paid before you get your share.	Although your money is safer than in individual stocks and shares, its value can still go down. Make sure you have enough savings elsewhere to cover most of your needs.
Investing in art, antiques, etc.	The risk depends on how much you know about the subject. Would you be able to spot a Rembrandt at a garage sale? If so, the risk in buying it would be low.	The reward also depends on you. If you thought it was a Rembrandt and it turned out not to be, you would have lost your money.	Only spend what you can afford to lose – unless you're 100% sure it is a Rembrandt.
Property	Most people buy property using a loan called a *mortgage*. If the value of the property falls, you can be left owing more money than the property is worth.	After many years you will have paid back the mortgage and will own the property. If it is your home, your housing costs will then be small.	Always make sure you can afford the mortgage repayments.

TAX AND INFLATION

However good you are at money management, there are two things affecting your money that you cannot control. The first is taxes, and the second is inflation. Each of these makes a real difference to both your earnings and your savings — and rarely in a good way.

What is tax?

Tax is a way of the government getting money. The money is then spent on things the government provides for it citizens. For example, tax money may be used to pay for our schools, armed forces, and healthcare.

The government gets tax money by taking a percentage of almost every financial exchange. For example, if you earn £1500.00 a month, the government might take 20% of it (or £300.00) as tax. This type of tax is called *income tax*, but there are many other kinds. For example:

- Sales tax is added to the cost of goods. If you buy a pen for 99p, for example, about 20p of that goes to the government.

Don't let your money slip away this easily!

- Death taxes are charged when someone dies. The government takes a percentage of their money before it is handed on to the dead person's heirs.

- Property taxes are charged to people who own a property. They are usually based on the value or size of the property.

What is inflation?

Inflation is the name for the way that prices go up over time. For example, if a steak cost £5.00 a year ago, but costs £5.50 today, its price has undergone inflation. Inflation is usually shown as a percentage. In the example, steak inflation is running at 10% a year, because the 50p increase is 10% of the old £5.00 price.

MONEY MATTERS

¥ $ £ € %

The inflationary basket
The general *inflation rate* is worked out using a range of different goods. This is often called a 'basket of goods' – the idea is that they are selected to reflect the things that most people regularly buy. The basket of goods might include milk, bread, chicken, washing powder, electricity, and washing machines, for example.

Inflation rates are based on the changing cost of an imaginary 'basket of goods'.

How does inflation affect your money?

Inflation affects your money in two main areas: earnings, and savings and investments:

Earnings

Inflation affects your earnings because, over time, it makes them worth less. Imagine you earn £25,000 a year, and are given a pay rise. Sounds good – but is it? You won't know without taking inflation into account:

Old salary:	New salary (with 5% pay rise):	Inflation at 3% of old salary:
£25,000	£26,250	£750

A 5% pay rise means you earn £1250 extra each year. If inflation is at 3%, you need to earn 3% more – £750 – to be able to afford the same things as last year. So your pay rise is *really* worth £500 (the extra £1250 minus £750).

Savings and investments

Inflation affects savings and investments in the same way as earnings. For example, you might earn 3% interest on your savings account. But if inflation is at 3% as well, the value of your money isn't really increasing, it is just staying the same.

THE P WORD – PENSIONS

If you hear someone say 'pensions', what do you think of (just before your eyes start to glaze over and you nod off to sleep)? Delete if appropriate: grey hair, false teeth, going bald, trousers with elastic waistbands, all-you-can-eat lunches, Saga holidays.

Doesn't look retired... doesn't look old enough — but with a bit of financial planning, perhaps you too could be free to ski into your 50s.

Fortunately, it doesn't have to be that way! How about this: waking up whatever time you like, going out for a coffee at 11, late lunch, then staying up till 2.30 a.m. because that one Steven Seagal movie you haven't yet seen is on Channel 5? Maybe you'll go snowboarding for a month in the winter, travel round Europe in your campervan in the summer, and get cheap flights everywhere because you can travel on a Wednesday morning?

To do this young enough to enjoy it, though, you need to think about a pension **RIGHT NOW**. Otherwise, you'll probably still be clocking on at B&Q four days a week at 75 years old.

What is a pension?
A pension is a scheme for providing people with income after they have stopped working. Usually they can only collect their pension payments when they get to a specific age. Some pensions reward people who put off, or defer, collecting their pensions until a later age.

How do pensions work?

Pensions work by collecting money from people who are working, in order to be able to pay out money in the future, when they have stopped working. The two main types of pension are state pensions and private pensions.

State pensions

In some countries, the government provides everyone with a small pension. The money is collected from working people's taxes. Most people are happy to pay in, knowing it means they get money out when they are older. State pensions provide enough money for basic survival, but little more.

Imagine the fun you'll have later if you start saving now.

Private pensions

Many people choose to be part of a private pension scheme. In this, they pay into a fund that is invested for them, which hopefully means their fund will grow. When they retire, the fund is used to provide a regular payment of money each month.

Self-planned pensions

Some people prefer to plan their own pension. For example, they might buy a second home, and aim to pay off the mortgage before they retire. The home can then be rented out, providing them with an income.

'I don't need to worry about pensions now – I'll think about that when I'm old.'
The trouble with that is, when you are old it will be too late. The sooner you start planning your pension, the more fun you will be able to have when you are older. Of course, that doesn't mean you can't have fun now as well!

43

TEST YOUR MONEY SKILLS

Having read this book, you probably understand more about the world of money and how it works than before. But how much has really sunk in? Run through our money-skills quiz to find out! (Note your answers on a sheet of paper, and check whether you were correct at the bottom of page 47.)

1) Why were bank notes first invented?
   a) So that money could be folded up and put in a wallet or purse.
   b) To help people trade safely in distant places.
   c) It gave the government a chance to put pictures of politicians on our money.

2) We all need money. But what decides the minimum amount you need each month?
   a) The rise or fall in the costs of new games for your Wii.
   b) The cost of food, clothing and somewhere to live.
   c) Whether or not Christmas is coming up and you have lots of presents to buy.

3) Which of these things can money get you?
   a) A fancy-looking convertible car.
   b) A big house with a swimming pool.
   c) Good friends.

4) How much money is enough?
   a) The same amount as my friends have.
   b) A little bit more than my friends.
   c) Enough to cover my own needs.

5) Where do most people learn their attitude to money?
   a) Their parents.
   b) Their teachers.
   c) Their friends.

6) You unexpectedly get given £100. What should you do with it?
   a) Spend it! After all, you weren't expecting it, so it's not 'real' money, is it?
   b) Put it all straight in your savings account and forget about it.
   c) It depends: if you already have some money saved up, and there's something you've been wanting to buy yourself for ages, then spend it. If you've just had to spend all your savings, because your bike was stolen, save it.

7) What is a money plan?
   a) A list of things you want to buy.
   b) A design for a new bank note.
   c) A way of working out how you can afford to buy something.

8) A budget is a way of working out if you have enough money coming in to cover your expenses. When your budget is unbalanced, what does it mean?
   a) You haven't spent all your money.
   b) Your spending is higher than your earnings.
   c) Your budget is a bit loony.

9) What's a good way to save money painlessly?
   a) Put 10% of everything you earn into a savings account.

Body Needs

VITAMINS and MINERALS
for a healthy body

Angela Royston

www.heinemann.co.uk/library

Visit our website to find out more information about **Heinemann Library** books.

To order:
☎ Phone 44 (0) 1865 888066
▤ Send a fax to 44 (0) 1865 314091
▢ Visit the Heinemann Bookshop at www.heinemann.co.uk/library to browse our catalogue and order online.

First published in Great Britain by Heinemann Library, Halley Court, Jordan Hill, Oxford OX2 8EJ, part of Harcourt Education. Heinemann is a registered trademark of Harcourt Education Ltd.

Editorial: Jilly Atwood and Jennifer Tubbs
Design: Ron Kamen and Celia Floyd
Illustrations: Geoff Ward
Picture Research: Catherine Bevan, Rosie Garai and Liz Eddison
Production: Séverine Ribierre

Originated by Ambassador Litho Ltd
Printed in China by Wing King Tong

ISBN 0 431 16712 5
07 06 05 04 03
10 9 8 7 6 5 4 3 2 1

British Library Cataloguing in Publication Data
Royston, Angela
Vitamins and Minerals
613.2'85
A full catalogue record for this book is available from the British Library.

Acknowledgements
The Publishers would like to thank the following for permission to reproduce photographs: Corbis: pp. **31**, **32** (Paul Barton), **33**, **36**; Gareth Boden: pp. **16**, **19**, **20**, **23**, **27**, **30**; Getty Images: pp. **4** (PPG International/Bill Losh), **7** (FPG International/VCL), **40** (FPG International/Gibson); Liz Eddison: pp. **8**, **9**, **28**; Photodisc: p. **6**; Roger Scruton: p. **10**; SPL: pp. **14** (B. O. Veisland, MI&I), **15** (Eye of Science), **17** (Prof. P. Motta/ Department of Anatomy/ University La Sapienza, Rome), **21** (Mark Clarke), **34** (Jim Varney), **35** (Biophoto Associates), **37** (John Paul Kay, Peter Arnold Inc.), **41** (Bettina Salomon).

Cover photograph of a strawberry and cream, reproduced with permission of Getty/Foodpix.

Every effort has been made to contact copyright holders of any material reproduced in this book. Any omissions will be rectified in subsequent printings if notice is given to the Publishers.

Contents

Fuelling the body machine 4

Vitamins and minerals 6

What are vitamins? 8

What are minerals? 10

Digesting vitamins and minerals 12

Absorbing vitamins and minerals 14

How the body uses vitamins 16

Using B vitamins and vitamin C 18

Using vitamins D, E and K 20

How the body uses minerals 22

Minerals in body fluids 24

Minerals in enzymes 26

Too much of a good thing 28

Too much salt and other minerals 30

Deficiency diseases 32

Other vitamin deficiencies 34

Mineral deficiencies 36

Healthy eating 38

Special requirements 40

Nutritional information 42

Glossary 44

Resources 47

Index 48

Any words appearing in the text in bold, **like this**, are explained in the glossary.

Fuelling the body machine

Your body works like a very complicated machine. Most machines involve electrical wiring, screws and bolts, but the body uses chemicals and chemical processes instead. In fact, most of the body's functions rely on different **chemical reactions**. Your body makes some of these chemicals itself, but it has to take in all the rest from the outside world – **oxygen** from the air and a wide range of chemicals from food. The chemicals that come from food are called **nutrients**.

Nutrients

The main nutrients in food are **carbohydrates**, **fats** and **proteins**. They supply your body with **energy** and the chemicals it needs to grow and replace **cells**. In addition to these main nutrients, your body needs small amounts of vitamins and minerals to help it carry out all the chemical processes that make it work. This book is about vitamins and minerals, but, since most foods contain a mixture of different kinds of nutrients, we shall take a look at the other nutrients first.

Carbohydrates

Foods such as bread, potatoes, pasta and rice contain lots of carbohydrates in the form of **starch**. The body changes the starch into sugar, which the muscles and other parts of your body use for energy. Sugar and foods that contain a lot of sugar, such as cakes, chocolate and sweets, are also rich in carbohydrates.

These basketball players are using up lots of energy as they throw the ball, run and jump. Most of their energy comes from eating foods that contain carbohydrates or fats.

Fats

Fats supply the body with energy, but in a more concentrated form than carbohydrates. If your body gets more carbohydrates and fats than it needs, it stores the surplus as a layer of fat under your skin and around **organs**, such as your heart.

Protein

Your body is made of millions of tiny cells. Different kinds of cells make up your skin, muscles and bones. Some cells do not last long before they have to be replaced. Cells consist mainly of water and protein, so to build new cells your body uses proteins that you get from foods such as meat, fish, eggs, beans and cheese. It is particularly important that children take in plenty of protein, because they are still growing and their bodies need it to make millions of extra cells.

This boy's height is being measured to see how tall he has grown. The protein in the cheese he is eating will help him to keep on growing.

Vitamins and minerals

The vast bulk of food consists of water and the main **nutrients** – **carbohydrates**, **fats** and **proteins** – but food also contains small amounts of vitamins and minerals. The fact that they only contain small amounts is fine, because your body only needs tiny amounts of each to stay healthy. The amounts are so small that most are measured as thousandth or hundredth parts of a gram. Nevertheless, without vitamins and minerals, you would soon become ill.

Too small to detect

Vitamins and minerals are needed in such small quantities that for centuries scientists did not know that most existed. They knew that to be healthy and to grow well, people needed to eat carbohydrates, fats, proteins and some minerals. And, since 1753, they had also known about the importance of fruit. Before then, sailors on long voyages often died of scurvy. This is a disease that stops wounds healing well and causes blood to leak from the tiny blood vessels under the skin and in the gums. A ship's doctor, called James Lind, thought that the sailors' limited diet, which did not include fruit or vegetables, might be causing the scurvy. He tried adding various foods, but the scurvy only stopped when he gave the sailors lemons and oranges.

Discovery of vitamins

About 150 years later, in 1906, a scientist called Frederick Hopkins experimented with the diet of rats. He discovered that 'astonishingly small amounts' of some substances are needed for the body to be able to use the main nutrients to grow and to thrive. Since then scientists have come to understand in detail how the body uses both vitamins and minerals. Some are needed by all the **cells** in the body, while others, like the vitamin C in lemon juice, work in particular kinds of cells. Vitamin C is needed to build strong blood vessels and to help wounds heal. This book is about the different vitamins and minerals and what happens if you eat too much or too little of any of them.

Lemons are a good source of vitamin C.

Minerals in the body

Calcium is the most common mineral in the body – about 1 per cent of your weight is calcium. So if you weigh 50 kilograms, you have about 500 grams of calcium in your body. There is much less of other minerals. Most adults, for example, have only about 3 to 4 grams of iron in their bodies.

Many foods contain small amounts of a few vitamins and minerals, so you need to eat a wide range of food, particularly vegetables and fruit, to get them all. The food in this shopping trolley will keep a whole family well supplied with vitamins and minerals for a week.

What are vitamins?

Vitamins are chemical **compounds** that contain carbon and various other elements and are found in plants and animals. We know of thirteen different vitamins that help our bodies carry out all the chemical processes needed to stay alive.

Identifying vitamins

Vitamins are sometimes known by their chemical names, but are often identified by a letter of the alphabet. For example, thiamin is often known as vitamin B_1 and ascorbic acid as vitamin C. Vitamins A, D, E and K **dissolve** in **fat** and are carried into the body mainly in fatty or oily food. The rest, the B vitamins and vitamin C, dissolve in water.

Vitamin A

The chemical name of vitamin A is retinol. Retinol itself is only found in animal foods, particularly liver and cod liver oil. But many fruits and vegetables also contain carotenes (yellow or orange substances), which can be converted in the body to retinal and so count towards vitamin A. The most important carotene is beta-carotene, which is found in carrots, red peppers, sweet potatoes, spinach and mangoes.

Most vitamins are found in a range of food. These foods are good sources of vitamins A, D, E or K, the vitamins that are soluble in fat.

Vitamin C and the B vitamins are **soluble** in water. These foods are rich in either the B vitamins or vitamin C. Some even have both.

B vitamins

Several different vitamins are included in a group called the B vitamins. They are grouped together because of the way the body uses them (see pages 18–19), but many are also found in the same foods. Milk, meat, cereals, bread and potatoes are good sources of several of the B vitamins. Vitamin B_{12} is more difficult to get. It is found only in food that comes from animals, such as meat, fish, eggs, cheese and milk.

Vitamin C

Vitamin C is found mainly in plants, including potatoes. In fact the only plants that do not contain vitamin C are cereals, dried peas and beans. You get much more vitamin C from eating fresh, raw fruit and vegetables than from cooked ones, since it is easily destroyed when it is heated or stored.

Making vitamins in the body

Although vitamins D and K are found in various foods, your body can make them itself. Vitamin D is sometimes called the 'sunshine vitamin' because when your skin is exposed to sunlight the vitamin forms in your skin. You take in some vitamin K from spinach, cabbage, cauliflower, peas and cereal. Vitamin K is also made inside your body, by bacteria in the large intestine.

What are minerals?

Minerals are **elements** that are found in the ground. They include iron, zinc, copper and other metals that are used in industry. But living things need minerals, too, although only in small amounts. Living things cannot make minerals and so have to take them in from the outside world. Your body needs about fifteen essential minerals to function and grow healthily. Some of these are particularly important and are called the major minerals. They are calcium, phosphorus, potassium, sodium, magnesium, iron and zinc.

These nails are made mainly of iron. This metal is needed by your body to help it function properly.

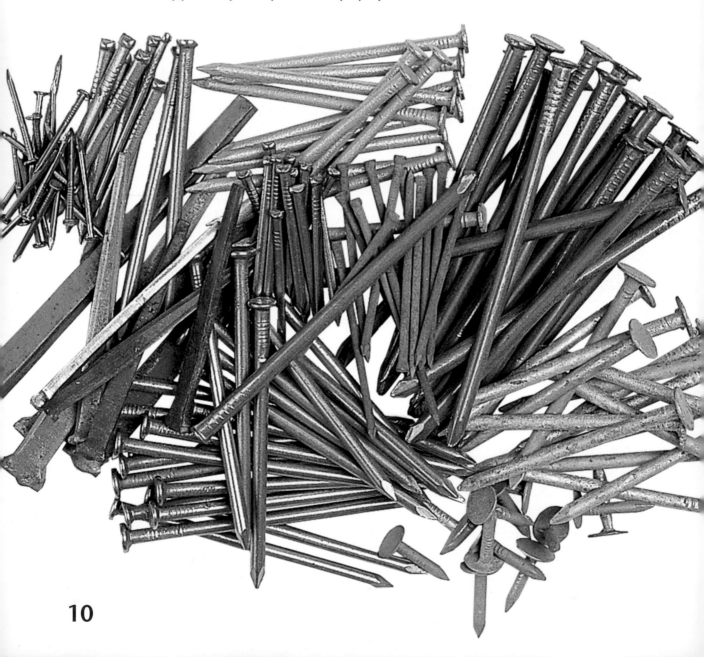

Trace elements

In addition to the eight major minerals, your body needs tiny amounts of seven other minerals, including copper, chromium, fluoride and iodine. We call these the **trace elements**. Apart from fluoride, these minerals are available in common foods. Fluoride makes teeth stronger and is added to most toothpastes and to some sources of tap water.

How we get minerals

Small amounts of minerals are scattered throughout the soil and some **dissolve** in water. Plants draw in water through their roots with these minerals dissolved in it. The minerals are taken to all parts of the plant and are then passed on to any animals that eat them, so almost all our food contains some minerals. The foods that are richest in the major minerals are milk, meat, bread and other cereals, and vegetables.

Milk and meat

Milk and dairy products such as cheese and yoghurt contain all the major minerals, although they are not a very good source of iron. Milk and cheese are especially rich in calcium, the mineral needed for strong bones and teeth. Meat, particularly liver, is the best source of iron, although other foods such as sardines, some fortified breakfast cereals and chocolate contain iron, too.

Bread, other cereals and plants

Bread and other cereal-based food, such as pasta and rice, contain all the major minerals, although less potassium than other minerals. Bananas and other fruit and vegetables are good sources of potassium. Some vegetables are particularly rich in certain minerals. Watercress and okra, for example, contain both calcium and iron, while potatoes are rich in magnesium and potassium.

Salt

Table salt is made up of two elements, sodium and chlorine, combined together. Salt is naturally present in most foods, while some foods, such as bacon, crisps, soy sauce and cornflakes, have a lot of salt added to them. In addition, many people add salt to the food they eat, although their normal diet contains plenty of salt already.

Digesting vitamins and minerals

Food contains the vitamins and minerals you need, but it has to be digested before your body can use them. The process of digestion breaks up food into smaller and smaller pieces. Digestion begins in your mouth and continues in your stomach and small intestine. Special chemicals called **enzymes** help to break down **carbohydrates**, **fats** and **proteins** into separate **molecules** and parts of molecules. Vitamins and minerals do not need to be broken down, but are taken into the blood with water or fats.

In the mouth

As you chew food, your teeth mash it up and mix it with **saliva** until it forms a soft, mushy lump. Then your tongue pushes it to the back of your mouth and you swallow it. It passes down your throat, through your **pharynx** into your **oesophagus**, and so into your stomach.

In the stomach

Your stomach is rather like a food blender. As it churns the food around and mixes it with digestive juice made in the wall of the stomach, the food slowly turns into a kind of thick soup, called **chyme**. The valve at the bottom of the stomach opens from time to time and a squirt of chyme passes to the small intestine, where the next stage occurs.

In the duodenum

The first part of the small intestine is called the **duodenum**. It is about 30 centimetres long and it is supplied with **bile** from the gall bladder and digestive juices from the walls of the small intestine and from the pancreas. Bile is made in the liver and stored in the gall bladder. It acts on fats in the same way as washing-up liquid does – bile breaks fats up into tiny globules or droplets so that it can be digested.

The rest of the small intestine

As the chyme passes through the small intestine it is swirled backwards and forwards. This helps the digestive juices to mix with the chyme and get to work. Digestive juices contain enzymes – special chemicals that the body makes to break fats, carbohydrates and proteins into smaller units. Fats take the longest to break up. It is not until they reach the end of the small intestine that most are absorbed into the blood.

Stomach facts

Your stomach stretches as it fills up with food. How long the food stays in the stomach depends on what it is and how much there is of it, but on average food stays in your stomach for about two to three hours.

The digestive system.

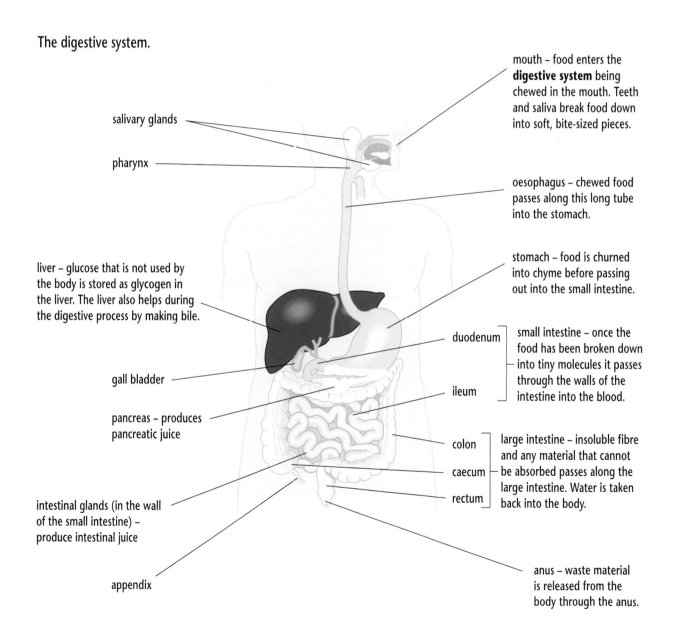

salivary glands

pharynx

mouth – food enters the **digestive system** being chewed in the mouth. Teeth and saliva break food down into soft, bite-sized pieces.

oesophagus – chewed food passes along this long tube into the stomach.

liver – glucose that is not used by the body is stored as glycogen in the liver. The liver also helps during the digestive process by making bile.

stomach – food is churned into chyme before passing out into the small intestine.

gall bladder

duodenum

ileum

small intestine – once the food has been broken down into tiny molecules it passes through the walls of the intestine into the blood.

pancreas – produces pancreatic juice

colon

caecum

rectum

large intestine – insoluble fibre and any material that cannot be absorbed passes along the large intestine. Water is taken back into the body.

intestinal glands (in the wall of the small intestine) – produce intestinal juice

appendix

anus – waste material is released from the body through the anus.

Absorbing vitamins and minerals

When **carbohydrates**, **fats** and **proteins** have been broken down into small enough pieces, they are ready to be absorbed into the blood. Most **nutrients**, including minerals and vitamins, are absorbed through the walls of the stomach and small intestine. Some pass through the liver, which processes and returns them to the blood for the rest of the body to use.

The villi

The walls of the small intestine are covered in tiny finger-like bumps called villi. Although the villi are extremely small – no more than half a millimetre long – they increase the surface area of the intestine wall considerably. This means the digested food has a greater chance of being absorbed. The walls of the villi are so thin that **molecules** of digested food pass through them and are absorbed into the tiny blood vessels inside.

Absorbing water

As food is broken down, the water in it is squeezed out. Water passes easily through the walls of the villi into the blood and carries with it whatever is **dissolved** in it. Minerals, vitamin C and some of the B vitamins are absorbed in the **duodenum**, the first part of the small intestine. More B vitamins are absorbed in the rest of the small intestine.

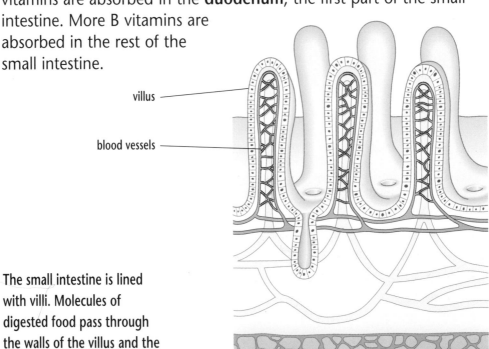

villus

blood vessels

The small intestine is lined with villi. Molecules of digested food pass through the walls of the villus and the blood vessels into the blood.

14

Absorbing fat-soluble vitamins

Bile breaks up fats into tiny droplets, which are then digested by **enzymes**. They break the large fat molecules into smaller units, called **fatty acids**. As the fatty acids are absorbed into the blood, the vitamins dissolved in them are absorbed too.

Not all vitamins and minerals are absorbed

Some vitamins and minerals are dependant on other factors being present for their absorption. For example, vitamin B_6 is needed for zinc to be absorbed, and vitamin C helps iron to be absorbed. Some foods, such as tea, coffee, rhubarb and wheat, contain substances that make it less likely that iron or other nutrients are absorbed.

The large intestine

Anything that is not absorbed in the small intestine passes through to the large intestine. Here millions of **bacteria** help to process the waste material. While this is happening, the bacteria manufacture vitamin K, which passes into the blood. At the same time, water passes from the undigested mush into the blood and the waste food, mixed with digestive juices, bacteria and other waste matter, slowly becomes more solid. This solid waste is pushed out of the body through the anus.

Bacteria in the large intestine manufacture vitamin K. The bacteria mix with the faeces, giving it its foul smell.

15

How the body uses vitamins

Vitamins are needed by all the millions of **cells** in the body and are essential for them to work properly. Most vitamins perform several different functions. Most do some work in all cells, but some vitamins work in particular kinds of cells. For example, folate, one of the B vitamins, is used in the **bone marrow** to produce new red blood cells.

Helping cells

Vitamins form part of many enzymes. This means that they are needed for **chemical change** to take place, but they are not part of the reaction. The main **nutrients** in food, for example, give your body **energy** and the materials to build new cells. But your body cannot use the main nutrients without the help of vitamins and minerals. They allow the cells to change fats and the sugar from **carbohydrates** into energy. Others help the cells to use **proteins** to build new cells and repair existing cells.

Defending against cancer

Some vitamins help to prevent free radical damage that can lead to cancer. As the body carries out its normal **chemical reactions** it produces chemicals called **free radicals**. Free radicals can damage protein and **DNA** in the body's cells. DNA is the **molecule** that contains your **genetic code** and tells your body how to build and repair itself. If the cells cannot repair the damage, they may become cancer cells. Vitamins C and E and some beta-carotenes combat these dangerous free radicals.

This girl is making herself a snack that is rich in carbohydrates, but her body cannot turn the carbohydrates into energy without the help of vitamins.

Preventing heart disease

A good intake of fruit and vegetables may be protective against certain diseases such as heart disease. Consuming a diet high in saturates can increase levels of LDL **cholesterol** (bad cholesterol) in the blood. It can accumulate in the vessel walls of the heart and become oxidised (damaged) causing the vessels to 'fur up' and narrow. Fruit and vegetables contain important vitamins and minerals and other substances, which act as **antioxidants** helping to prevent the oxidation of LDL cholesterol.

Vitamin A

Vitamin A makes your skin, hair and nails healthy, but it does not work if you rub it into your hair or skin. Vitamins only work from inside the body. Vitamin A also helps children to grow well. It does this because the body needs it to produce new cells.

Seeing in the dark

Carrots really do help you see in the dark. They do not give you night vision, but they are rich in vitamin A. The cells in your eyes need vitamin A to help them detect dim light. Without it, you would be blind at night.

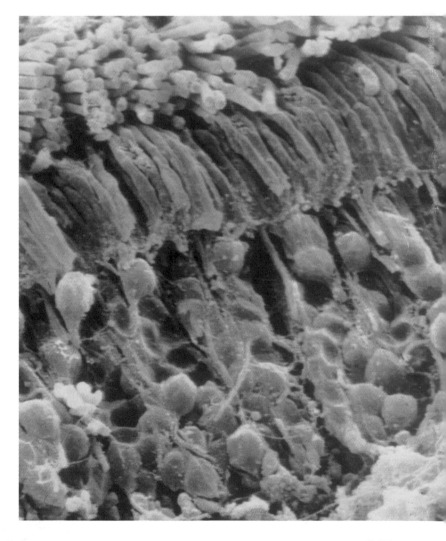

This is what the cells in your eyes that react to dim light look like under a microscope. The purple colour is due to vitamin A. When light hits these cells the purple changes to white and this chemical change triggers the nerves that allow you to see.

Using B vitamins and vitamin C

Both B vitamins and vitamin C are **soluble** in water. You need a constant supply of them, because your body cannot store them. Some B vitamins help your **cells** change food into **energy**, while others build up new **proteins**. Vitamin C helps to keep your skin, bones and other tissues healthy.

Releasing energy from food

The B vitamins thiamin, riboflavin and niacin are all needed by the cells to release energy from food. Thiamin works only on **carbohydrates**, while riboflavin helps to release the energy in **fats** and proteins as well as carbohydrates. Two more B vitamins – pantothenic acid and biotin – are essential for your body to use the energy in fats.

Using protein

During digestion, protein in your food is broken down into units called **amino acids**. Vitamin B_6 helps your cells rebuild the amino acids into new proteins. One of these proteins is **haemoglobin**, the substance that makes red blood cells red. Haemoglobin takes in **oxygen** from the air you breathe in and carries it to the rest of the body. Vitamin B_6 can also manufacture the B vitamin niacin from one of the amino acids.

Vitamin B_{12} and folate

These two B vitamins are needed in parts of the body where cells are being made very quickly. For example, your **bone marrow** – the soft jelly in the middle of some bones – manufactures about 100 million new red blood cells every minute. It cannot manage this without vitamin B_{12} and folate. Both of these vitamins also help to form healthy nerve cells.

Cook your eggs

Egg yolks contain the B vitamin biotin, but your body can only use it if the egg is cooked. Otherwise a substance contained in raw egg white combines with biotin and prevents the body using it.

18

Connective tissue

Vitamin C is needed to produce collagen, the substance that forms the structure of your skin, bones, teeth and connective tissue. Connective tissue is strong but stretchy. It keeps your heart, lungs, stomach and so on in place, but allows them to move as you bend, twist and stretch. Other examples of connective tissue include gums, which hold your teeth in your jaws; tendons, which attach your muscles to your bones; and ligaments which hold your joints together.

Other uses of vitamin C

Vitamin C builds strong blood vessels and helps wounds to heal. Vitamin C also helps with the absorption of iron from foods other than meat.

Guava, oranges, West Indian cherries and blackcurrants are just some of the fruits that are particularly rich in vitamin C. Eating them will help to keep this girl's gums, teeth and other tissues healthy.

Using vitamins D, E and K

Vitamins D, E and K, like vitamin A, are all **soluble** in **fat**. This means that the body can store them. Each one has a particular function in the body.

Vitamin D

The main task of vitamin D is to help your body absorb the mineral calcium. Much of the vitamin D in your body is made by sunlight acting on your skin, but if you usually keep your skin covered, you need to take in the vitamin from food. The liver and the kidneys process vitamin D. They turn it into a substance that controls the amount of calcium that is absorbed into the blood through your **digestive system**.

Calcium in the bones

Calcium also needs vitamin D after it has been absorbed into the blood. Most of the calcium you eat is deposited in your bones and teeth, where it makes them strong and rigid. But scientists think that without vitamin D, your bones and teeth cannot take the calcium in.

This girl is getting vitamin D from two sources – from the yoghurt and from sunlight on her skin. It will help the calcium in the yoghurt form strong bones and teeth.

Vitamin E

Vitamin E is most important in the body as an **antioxidant**. This means that it helps to prevent damage by the chemicals called **free radicals** that can cause cancer and heart disease. At the same time, vitamin E has several other functions. These functions include its structural role in cells. It is also needed by the immune system.

Vitamin K

This vitamin helps blood to clot and wounds to heal. If you cut yourself, blood flows from the tiny blood vessels in your skin. Several chemicals make the blood in the wound become thicker and form a clot. The clot plugs the wound and hardens to form a scab, which protects the wound while the blood vessels heal and new skin grows.

Blood facts

Blood can carry the **bacteria** and viruses that cause serious diseases. If you help someone with a cut, don't let their blood touch your skin or get inside your body. Always cover cuts with a clean dressing or plaster.

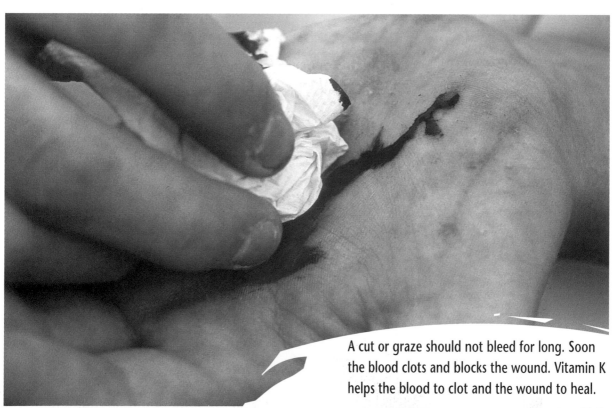

A cut or graze should not bleed for long. Soon the blood clots and blocks the wound. Vitamin K helps the blood to clot and the wound to heal.

How the body uses minerals

Minerals are used throughout the body, both inside and outside the **cells**. They have three main functions. Some make your bones and teeth strong and rigid. Others become part of your cells and body fluids, such as blood and sweat. The rest are needed to make **enzymes**, the substances that help your cells carry out **chemical reactions**.

Bones

The minerals that make bones and teeth hard are calcium, phosphorus and magnesium. Your bones use 99 per cent of the calcium, 75 per cent of the phosphorus and half of the magnesium in your body. Without them, your bones would still be strong, but they would be bendy like cartilage – the substance that you can feel at the tips of your ears.

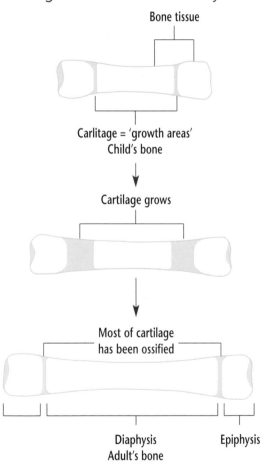

Bone tissue

Carlitage = 'growth areas'
Child's bone

Cartilage grows

Most of cartilage
has been ossified

Diaphysis   Epiphysis
Adult's bone

A child's bone contains much more cartilage than an adult's bone. As the cartilage absorbs minerals and changes into bone, the child's bone slowly grows and new cartilage forms at the ends.

Calcium store

Calcium can move in and out of your bones if it is needed elsewhere. Muscles work by contracting, that is, by getting shorter, but they need calcium to be able to do this. Your heart is a muscle and it needs calcium, too. Bones act as a store of calcium in case your body is not taking in enough from food.

Absorbing calcium

Your body takes in less than half the amount of calcium your food contains. Several factors can reduce this amount even further. You need vitamin D in order to absorb calcium and deposit it in your bones, so if you are lacking in vitamin D you will take in less calcium. Some foods, particularly spinach and rhubarb, contain chemicals that stop calcium being absorbed into the blood. This does not mean that you should never eat spinach and rhubarb, but that you should eat calcium-rich food separately.

Fluoride

Fluoride is a **trace element** (see page 11) that makes your teeth less likely to decay. **Bacteria** in your mouth feed on sugar and produce a strong acid that dissolves enamel, the hard coating on your teeth. Once the acid has made a hole in the enamel of a tooth, it can eat its way through the **dentine** below, causing your tooth to rot. Fluoride works best on your teeth while they are still forming. Your milk teeth form before you are born, but your adult teeth are slowly forming until you are about ten years old.

Using toothpaste that contains flouride helps to prevent your teeth decaying.

Dissolving bone

If you put a chicken bone in a container with vinegar and leave it, the minerals in the bone will slowly **dissolve**. After a few weeks the bone will have become bendy, like the cartilage it formed from.

Minerals in body fluids

Your body is awash with liquid. Apart from blood, sweat, tears and other body fluids, every **cell** contains liquid. These fluids are mainly water with minerals and other substances **dissolved** in them. Minerals in the water inside and outside your cells control what passes into and out of the cells. Salt, containing the **elements** sodium and chlorine, helps to control the amount of water in your body.

Salt in the body

All your body fluids, including blood, urine, tears, mucus and sweat contain salt. The amounts of salt and other minerals in your body are controlled by your kidneys. They make sure that the concentration of salt in your blood stays about the same. If your blood contains extra salt, you will feel thirsty and drink extra water. If you eat very salty crisps, for example, you will become thirsty. If your blood is low in salt, your kidneys get rid of extra water to keep the concentration of salt about the same.

Chloe's story

Chloe was feeling very cross and tired. It had been particularly hot weather for several weeks and she kept getting cramp in her legs. She knew she should drink extra water in hot weather, but she didn't realize that sweating had left her body short of salt. Then one night she and a friend shared a huge packet of salty crackers. Chloe was amazed to find she no longer felt tired and the cramps went away, too.

Sweat

If you lick your skin when you have been sweating, it will taste salty. Sweating helps to control the temperature of the body. At the same time your body loses water and minerals, particularly salt. If the weather is very hot, or if you have been sweating due to exercise, you should take in extra water and salt, to make up for that lost.

Border crossing

Blood carries the **nutrients** from digested food to every cell in your body. Each cell is surrounded by salty water. The liquid inside each cell, however, contains potassium, magnesium and phosphorus. The difference between these liquids allows nutrients and **oxygen** to pass from the blood into the cell. It also allows waste chemicals, such as **proteins** and **carbon dioxide** to pass from the cell into the blood. The blood carries the waste away to be later expelled from the body.

About two-thirds of your body is water. In an adult this includes about 4.5 litres of blood, 3 litres of digestive juices and about 250 millilitres of urine. The rest is liquid in and around the cells and internal tubes.

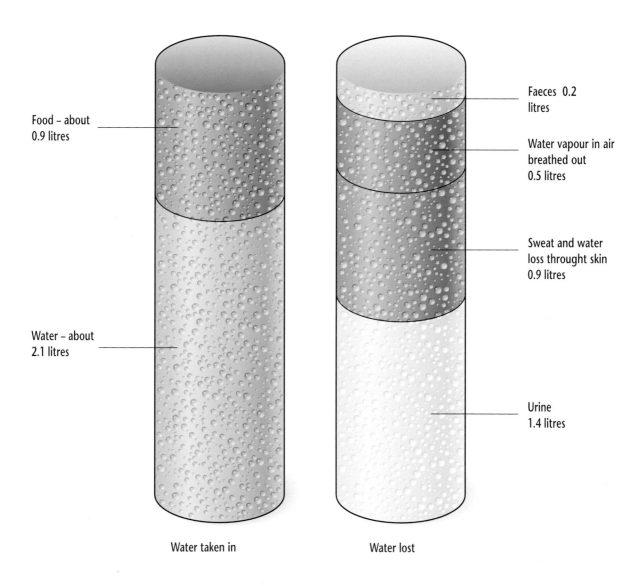

Food – about 0.9 litres

Water – about 2.1 litres

Faeces 0.2 litres

Water vapour in air breathed out 0.5 litres

Sweat and water loss throught skin 0.9 litres

Urine 1.4 litres

Water taken in

Water lost

Your body takes in and loses water every day. Salt in the body helps to keep a balance between the water you take in and the water lost.

Minerals in enzymes

Minerals and some vitamins form part of many **enzymes**. We have already seen how enzymes work in the **digestive system** (see page 12), but enzymes also act inside every single body **cell**. A single cell may have hundreds of reactions going on at the same time, each using a different enzyme. Enzymes speed up the rate at which chemicals react, and cells would not be able to survive without them.

Taking in oxygen

More than half the iron in your body is in your blood. It is contained in **haemoglobin**, the red substance in red blood cells. As blood passes through the lungs, **oxygen** from the air you breathe in becomes attached to haemoglobin. Later, as the blood is pumped around the body, the oxygen leaves the haemoglobin and passes into the cells.

Losing carbon dioxide

Oxygen combines with sugar to produce **energy** inside the cell. As it does so, **carbon dioxide** is produced. This gas passes out of the cell and attaches itself to haemoglobin that has lost its oxygen. The carbon dioxide leaves the blood in the lungs and is breathed out.

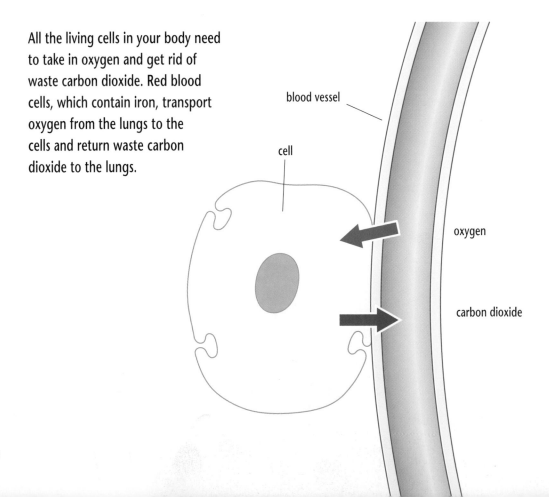

All the living cells in your body need to take in oxygen and get rid of waste carbon dioxide. Red blood cells, which contain iron, transport oxygen from the lungs to the cells and return waste carbon dioxide to the lungs.

blood vessel

cell

oxygen

carbon dioxide

Iron in the body

What happens to the rest of the iron in your body? Some of it is used by the muscles, and the rest is stored in your liver. Other animals store iron in their liver too, which makes eating liver a good source of this mineral. When red blood cells die, the iron in the haemoglobin is reused, so your body loses iron only when you lose blood. Iron is not easily absorbed into the body and needs vitamin C for even a quarter of the iron in food to pass into the blood.

Zinc

Zinc, like iron, is a major mineral (see page 10). It works with many different enzymes. It is needed for children to grow and for their bodies to become sexually mature at **puberty**. In addition, zinc helps wounds to heal.

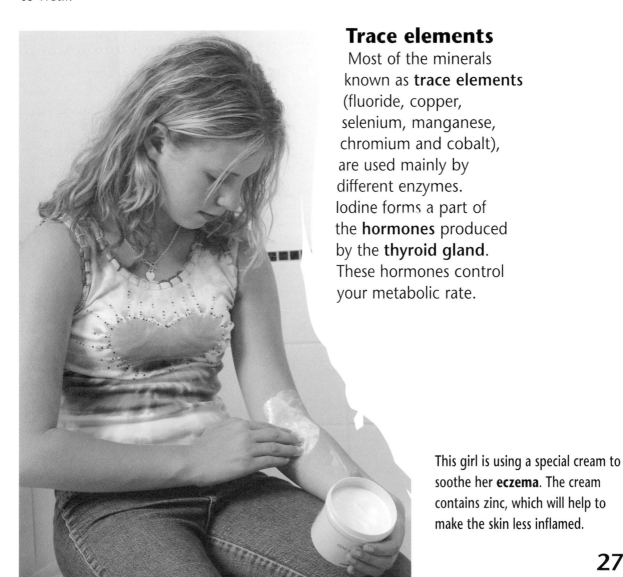

Trace elements

Most of the minerals known as **trace elements** (fluoride, copper, selenium, manganese, chromium and cobalt), are used mainly by different enzymes. Iodine forms a part of the **hormones** produced by the **thyroid gland**. These hormones control your metabolic rate.

This girl is using a special cream to soothe her **eczema**. The cream contains zinc, which will help to make the skin less inflamed.

Too much of a good thing

Your body needs so little of each vitamin and mineral that swallowing vitamin and mineral pills can easily give your body much more than it needs. Too much of some vitamins and minerals can harm you.

Supplements

Many supplements are sold as cures for various conditions, or simply to make you extra healthy. Normally, if you eat a wide variety of food, you will get plenty of each kind of vitamin and mineral. In some cases, however, supplements can be useful (see pages 40 and 41).

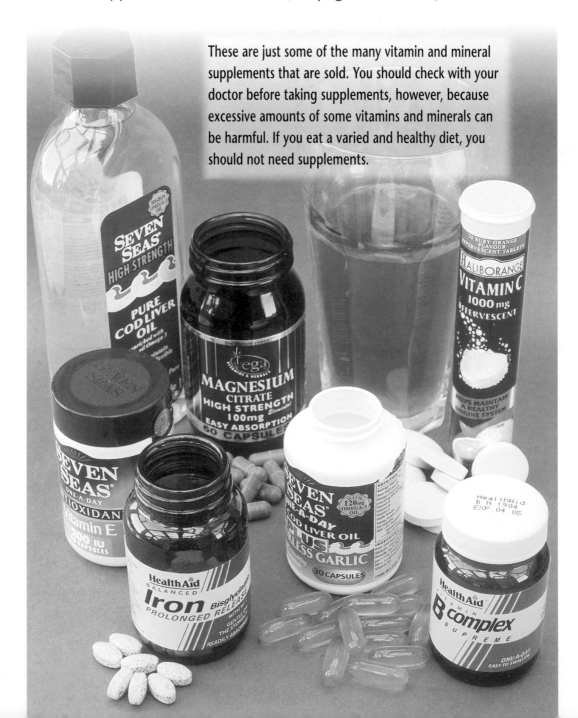

These are just some of the many vitamin and mineral supplements that are sold. You should check with your doctor before taking supplements, however, because excessive amounts of some vitamins and minerals can be harmful. If you eat a varied and healthy diet, you should not need supplements.

Can vitamin C cure colds?

Some people take up to 250 times the recommended amount of vitamin C, claiming that it can cure the common cold. Most scientists disagree and say that there is no evidence to support such a claim.

Water-soluble vitamins

It does not matter if you have too much vitamin C or most B vitamins. They are **soluble** in water, and any extra is just filtered by your kidneys into your urine. There are a few exceptions to this, however. If you take too much niacin, one of the B vitamins, it can make your face and hands feel as if they are burning and it can damage your liver. Too much Vitamin B_6 can harm your sensory nerves – the nerves that carry signals to your brain from your senses.

Fat-soluble vitamins

If you take in more fat-soluble vitamins that your body needs, your liver stores the excess. This means that if your diet is short of vitamins A, D, E or K for a short time, your body will simply draw on supplies from the liver. Taking in much too much of vitamins E or K, does not harm you, but too much of vitamins A or D can.

Too much vitamin A

If you take in too much vitamin A, the extra can poison your liver. Unborn babies are most at risk from being damaged by too much vitamin A. Pregnant women should avoid eating liver, or things made of liver, such as liverwurst or pâté, because the excessive amounts of vitamin A in liver can cause **birth defects** in their babies.

Too much vitamin D

Vitamin D controls how much calcium is absorbed into the body, so too much vitamin D can lead to an excess of calcium. Extra calcium is usually filtered out in your urine, but, if there is more than your kidneys can cope with, the extra can damage them. Young children, in particular, should not add too much vitamin D to their diets.

Too much salt and other minerals

If you eat a balanced diet you will get enough – but not too much – of most minerals. However, many people eat more salt than they need, and this gives some people health problems. Babies are particularly at risk from too much salt or phosphorus, while too much fluoride can discolour your teeth.

Added salt

There is enough natural salt in food to supply our needs, but salt makes food tastier and it is usually added when food is cooked. In addition we often sprinkle more salt on to the food on our plates. Scientists calculate that, on average, most people eat twice the amount of salt they need and some eat even more.

High blood pressure

If your blood contains extra salt, your kidneys filter out much of the extra. But the kidneys also keep extra water in the blood to balance the excess salt. This increases the volume of blood in your body and can cause high blood pressure. Blood pressure measures the force with which the heart pumps blood into the **arteries**. High blood pressure can damage the heart, cause **strokes** and damage the kidneys. Children who eat too much salt are more likely to suffer from high blood pressure when they are older.

This packet of crisps contains 385 milligrams of sodium, that is 1 gram of salt – about a quarter of all the salt you need in a day. Peanuts and other salty snacks, bacon and many precooked foods are very high in salt.

Mercury in fish

Large fish, particularly swordfish, shark and marlin, have high levels of mercury in their flesh. The mercury is washed off the land into the sea. Mercury damages the nervous system so children under sixteen years old and pregnant women should not eat these fish.

Babies

A baby's kidneys cannot get rid of extra salt, which then damages their kidneys. Extra salt should never be added to a baby's food until they are at least a year old. There is enough natural salt in food to supply them with all the sodium and chlorine they need. Newborn babies must be fed on breast milk or special formula milk, because ordinary cow's milk contains too much phosphorus for them.

Too much fluoride

Extra fluoride makes your teeth strong and less likely to need fillings (see page 23), but some children receive more fluoride than they need. Most brands of toothpaste contain fluoride, and, in some places, fluoride is added to the tap water. You should not take fluoride tablets if fluoride is already added to the drinking water. Extra fluoride will make your teeth extra strong, but it may discolour them.

Fluoride is added to some drinking water. Too much of it can discolour your teeth.

Deficiency diseases

Eating a balanced and varied diet gives your body all the vitamins and minerals you need. However, people who do not get enough of just one of these essential **nutrients** can suffer from a range of problems. A shortage of a particular vitamin or mineral can cause one of many deficiency diseases.

Who suffers from deficiency diseases?

Some people have a medical condition that makes it hard for them to absorb a particular vitamin or mineral. Other people eat such a limited diet that they deprive their bodies of essential nutrients. But the people who are most likely to suffer from deficiency diseases are the millions of people throughout the world who are starving or who cannot afford to eat a good diet. Even in rich countries, there are many, particularly elderly people or very poor people, who cannot afford to feed themselves properly.

Effects of deficiency diseases

Vitamins and minerals each perform many different functions in the body. So, a deficiency disease usually affects the body in a number of different ways. The person's body does not work well and they often feel ill and weak. Their skin, muscles, blood or bones may be particularly affected.

Old people are more at risk of developing some deficiency diseases than younger people. As people get older more effort needs to be made to stay fit and healthy.

Body stores

Your body stores some minerals and vitamins, particularly the vitamins that are **soluble** in fats. Your liver, for example, can store enough vitamin D to last you for two years.

This person is suffering from pellagra, caused by a lack of the B vitamin, niacin. The skin around the neck has become sore and irritated.

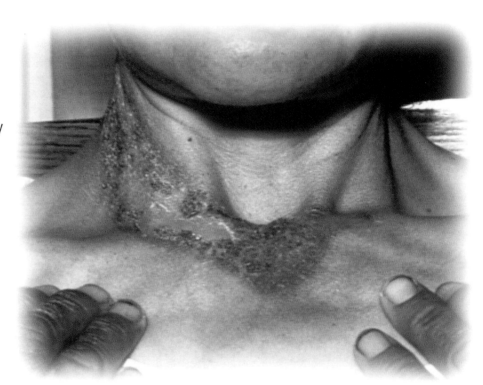

Pellagra

Pellagra is caused by a lack of niacin and other B vitamins. It is common among people who eat mainly corn (also called maize), since it does not contain much niacin. People feel weak, but not hungry, and they suffer from indigestion and **diarrhoea**. Their skin becomes irritated, dark and scaly, particularly where it is exposed to sunlight.

Beriberi

This disease is caused by a lack of the B vitamin thiamin in the diet. It used to be common in China, Japan and South-east Asia where people ate 'polished' rice, which is rice that contains no thiamin. The name of the disease means 'I cannot' and describes how sufferers become too sick to do anything. Their legs become stiff, paralysed and painful. Today man-made thiamin is added to white rice, and the disease has become less common.

Other vitamin deficiencies

Too little vitamin A

A deficiency of vitamin A affects the nerve endings in the eyes that detect dim light. This makes it hard to see in the dark and can lead to a person being blind at night. A lack of vitamin A also makes it harder for your body to fight off **infectious** diseases, and can make you grow more slowly.

Too little B vitamins

Because your body cannot store B vitamins, a shortage of them can affect your health after just a few months. Apart from beriberi and pellagra (see page 33), a shortage of vitamin B_{12} or of folate can cause **anaemia**. Anaemia means that the person does not have enough healthy red blood **cells** to keep their cells supplied with **oxygen**. It makes them feel tired and lacking in energy.

Too little vitamin C

A shortage of vitamin C can cause a lack of iron (see page 37). In extreme cases, lack of vitamin C stops the body from being able to heal. This condition is called scurvy. The small blood vessels that supply your cells become weak and blood spills out under the skin. It is particularly noticeable in the gums and mouth, which both become sore. The person's gums bleed and their teeth become loose.

Scientists use microscopes to check whether a sample of blood is anaemic. They count the number of healthy red blood cells in the sample.

Rickets is a disease that can make you bowlegged. It is caused by eating food that lacks vitamin D or calcium when you are young.

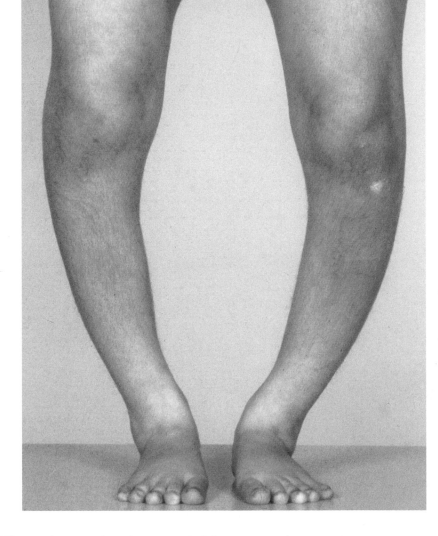

Too little vitamin D

Since vitamin D controls how much calcium your body absorbs and uses, a lack of vitamin D leads to a lack of calcium. Children need plenty of vitamin D and calcium because their bones are still growing. If they do not get enough, they may develop rickets. This means that their bones do not grow strong and straight.

Too little vitamin E

Your body stores vitamin E in the fat that lies under your skin. It is unlikely that your diet will lack vitamin E. The only people who are at risk are people whose bodies cannot absorb the vitamin and **premature** babies. Babies that are born early have very little body fat and so very little stored vitamin E. Unless they are given extra vitamin E they become anaemic.

Too little vitamin K

A shortage of vitamin K means that the blood does not clot properly. So, if you cut yourself, the wound will bleed much more and for far longer than it should. This deficiency is very unlikely to happen, however, because your body constantly makes vitamin K in your large intestine. A small number of newborn babies are short of the vitamin, so babies are usually given extra vitamin K as soon as they are born.

Mineral deficiencies

Too little calcium

Children and young adults need to eat plenty of foods that contains calcium. Children who do not get enough calcium may develop rickets. After a person has stopped growing calcium is continued to be laid down in the bones until peak bone mass is reached, People who do not reach their peak bone mass when they are younger are at risk of developing osteoporosis when they are older. This is a condition that makes bones break easily.

Too little salt

If you often get muscle cramps, you may be suffering from lack of salt, particularly if the weather is hot or you often take part in sports that make you sweat. When you sweat, your body loses salt as well as water. You may feel thirsty but you may not realize that you also have to replace the salt you have lost. Lack of salt can make you feel tired and sick as well.

Runners drink special sports drinks that contain salt as well as water. It replaces the salt they lose through sweating.

David's grandmother's story

David's grandmother broke her leg and her arm when she tripped over a rug in her home. The fall was not bad, but, like many elderly women, she suffers from osteoporosis. Her bones have lost a lot of calcium and have become very brittle. Once the calcium has been lost, old people cannot replace it. David's mother is determined that she will not suffer from osteoporosis when she is older. She is planning to keep exercising and to eat foods that contain plenty of calcium.

Too little potassium or magnesium

The people most likely to be deficient in these minerals are those who are suffering from a disease called kwashiorkor, caused by a lack of **protein**. Diseases that cause severe and long-lasting **diarrhoea** may also lead to a shortage of potassium or magnesium. If this happens, the person may have a heart attack and die.

Too little iron

A shortage of iron is one of the most common causes of **anaemia**. Lack of iron means that the body cannot produce **haemoglobin** and so leads to a shortage of red blood **cells**. Not having enough red blood cells stops cells in your body getting all the oxygen they need.

Too little iodine

People who do not get enough iodine in their diet suffer from a disease of the **thyroid gland** known as goitre. The gland swells up, and their neck can become huge.

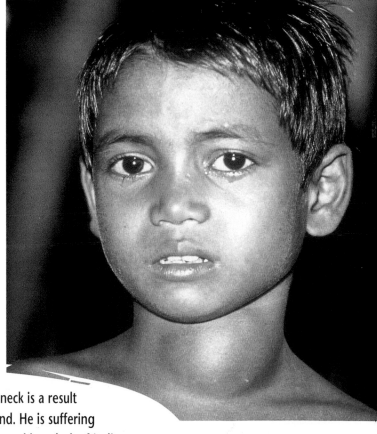

The swelling on this boy's neck is a result of an enlarged thyroid gland. He is suffering from goitre, a condition caused by a lack of iodine.

Healthy eating

Provided you eat a varied diet you should get all the vitamins and minerals you need. Any kind of food contains only small amounts of some vitamins and minerals, so you need to eat many different kinds of food to make sure that you get all of them. As well as a varied diet you also need to eat a balanced diet. The 'Balance of Good Health' plate shows you how much you should eat of different kinds of food.

1 – Bread, cereals and potatoes

This group includes rice, pasta, breakfast cereals as well as bread, potatoes and yams. These foods all contain a lot of **carbohydrates** and will keep your body supplied with **energy**. They also contain many vitamins and minerals. About a third of all the food you eat in a day should come from this group.

2 – Fruit and vegetables

This group is rich in vitamins and minerals and in **fibre**. Fibre is the part of the food that your body cannot digest so you might think it is unimportant. In fact it is essential for your **digestive system** to work efficiently. Another third of your food should come from this group.

3 – Meat, fish and alternatives

This group includes eggs and pulses and is rich in **proteins**, which your body needs to repair and build new **cells**. You need to eat about two to three portions of this food each day. Meat, fish and eggs come from animals and are particularly rich in B vitamins and iron as well as protein. Beans and pulses are low in fat.

4 – Milk and dairy foods

This group includes cheese, yoghurt and all other foods made from milk. These foods provide proteins, **fats**, fat-**soluble** vitamins (A, D, E and K) and many minerals, particularly calcium.

5 – Foods containing fat or sugar

This group of foods includes crisps, sweets, chocolate, fizzy drinks and the sweet snacks and treats that most children enjoy. Some of these foods are also high in salt. To be healthy, you should eat only a very small amount of these foods each day.

Rules for healthy eating
- Eat a wide variety of food.
- Eat most food from groups 1 and 2.
- Eat only a little food from group 5.

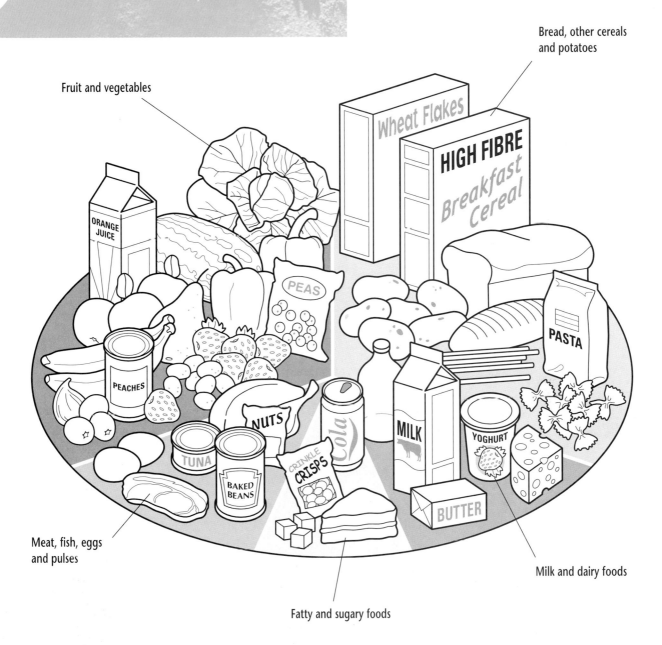

Bread, other cereals and potatoes

Fruit and vegetables

Meat, fish, eggs and pulses

Fatty and sugary foods

Milk and dairy foods

This plate of food shows the 'Balance of Good Health'. It divides food into five groups and shows the proportion of your diet that should come from each group.

Special requirements

While most people can get all the vitamins and minerals they need by eating a varied and balanced diet, some groups of people need to take extra vitamins or minerals. They can do this by choosing foods that are rich in the **nutrients** they need, or by taking supplements in the form of vitamin and mineral pills.

Vegans

Vegetarian diets include dairy foods and contain all the vitamins and minerals you need, but vegans do not eat any food that comes from animals at all. They have to plan their diet carefully to make sure that it does not lack vitamin B$_{12}$. They can take this vital vitamin in the form of a vitamin pill.

Pregnant women

When a woman is pregnant, her body diverts resources to the baby growing inside her, so that she has to make sure she takes in enough for herself, too. In particular, she needs extra iron, calcium and vitamins

C and D so the baby can build strong bones and red blood **cells**. Pregnant women are usually given extra folate, or folic acid, to protect their unborn babies from a condition called **spina bifida**. Pregnant women should avoid liver because it is very rich in vitamin A; too much vitamin A can cause **birth defects**. They should also avoid certain fish (see page 31).

During pregnancy, women must eat food that contains plenty of vitamins and minerals and avoid eating liver and certain fish.

Babies and young children

Babies get all the nutrients they need from their mother's breast milk. Once breast-feeding has stopped, however, it is important that they receive a nourishing diet that includes all the vitamins they need, but not extra salt (see page 30). Many babies and young children are given drops that contain extra vitamins A, C and D.

Old people

As people grow older, they tend to eat less. They have to take extra care to make sure they are receiving sufficient amounts of all nutrients, including vitamins and minerals. Elderly people who do not go outside cannot make vitamin D from sunlight and may lack this vitamin so they should eat foods poviding vitamin D.

Athletes

Athletes are usually very careful about the food they eat and make sure their bodies are fit and healthy. However, if they take part in endurance events or sports that make them sweat a lot for many hours, they have to drink extra liquid during the event. Special sports drinks contain extra salt to replace that lost in sweating.

This baby is learning to feed himself. Parents must make sure that the food their children eat is healthy. Many baby foods have vitamins and minerals specially added to them.

Nutritional information

The two tables on this page show how much of some vitamins and minerals you should have every day. Some food labels tell you how much sodium the food contains. Salt is sodium chloride so the figure for sodium tells you how much salt is in the food. It is recommended that adults should have no more than 2.3 grams (2300 milligrams) of sodium per day, that is, about 6 grams of salt.

Recommended daily requirements of some vitamins

A µg (microgram) is one millionth of a gram.
An mg (milligram) is one thousandth of a gram.

Age	A (µg)	B_1 (mg)	B_{12} (µg)	Folate (µg)	C (mg)	D (µg)
7–10	500	0.7	1.0	150	30	5–15
11–14 (girls)	600	0.7	1.2	200	35	10–15
11–14 (boys)	600	0.9	1.2	200	35	10–15

Recommended daily amounts of some minerals

Age	Calcium (mg)	Iron (mg)	Zinc (mg)	Sodium (mg)
7–10	550	8.7	7.0	1200
11–19 (girls)	800	14.8	9.0	1600
11–19 (boys)	1000	11.3	9.5	1600

Extra vitamin C
When your body is under stress, it uses up vitamin C faster. Smoking puts your body under constant stress, so smokers need to take in up to three times the normal recommended amount of vitamin C.

This table shows how many milligrams (mg) of some vitamins and minerals are contained in 100 grams of different foods. (A thousand milligrams make a gram.)

Food (100g portion)	Thiamin (mg)	Vit C (mg)	Calcium (mg)	Iron (mg)	Sodium (mg)
Spaghetti (boiled and unsalted)	0.01	0	7	0.50	0
Boiled rice	0.01	0	18	0.20	1
White bread	0.21	0	110	1.60	3
Cornflakes	1.00	0	15	6.70	1,110
Baked potatoes	0.37	14	11	0.70	12
Raw cabbage	0.15	49	52	0.70	5
Cucumber	0.03	2	18	0.30	3
Boiled spinach	0.06	6	150	1.70	16
Watercress	0.16	62	170	2.20	49
Apples	0.03	6	4	0.10	3
Blackcurrants	0.02	130	51	1.10	2
Dates	0.07	1	230	3.90	10
Oranges	0.11	54	47	0.10	5
Strawberries	0.03	77	16	0.40	6
Baked beans	0.09	0	53	1.40	530
Grilled back bacon	0.43	0	12	1.50	2,020
Stewed minced beef	0.05	0	18	3.10	320
Canned sardines	0.04	0	550	2.90	650
Whole milk	0.03	1	115	0.06	55
Cheddar cheese	0.03	0	720	0.30	670
Low fat fruit yoghurt	0.05	1	150	0.10	64
Chocolate	0.10	0	220	1.60	120
Chocolate biscuits	0.03	0	110	1.70	160

Glossary

amino acids   chemical building-blocks that make up proteins

anaemia   when a person does not have enough healthy red blood cells to keep their cells supplied with oxygen

antioxidant   substance that helps to neutralize the chemicals called free radicals that can cause cancer and heart disease

arteries   tubes that carry blood from the heart to different parts of the body

bacteria   single, living cells. Most kinds of bacteria are harmless, but some kinds can cause disease.

bile   green liquid made in the liver which breaks up the fats in food

birth defects   physical problems or conditions that are present when a baby is born

bone marrow   jelly-like substance in the centre of some bones. Red and white blood cells are manufactured in the bone marrow.

carbohydrates   substances in food that your body uses to provide energy. Foods that contain carbohydrates include bread, rice, potatoes, and sugar.

carbon dioxide   one of the gases in the air. Animals breathe out carbon dioxide.

cell   smallest living unit. The body is made up of many different kinds of cells, such as bone cells, blood cells and skin cells.

chemical change   joining of two substances to produce a different substance, or the splitting up of a substance into two or more different substances

chemical reaction   process that occurs when substances undergo chemical change

cholesterol   fatty substance found in some foods and in most parts of your body, including the blood

chyme   mushy liquid which passes from the stomach to the small intestine. It is formed from partly digested food mixed with the digestive juices of the stomach

compound   substance made up of two or more simple substances

dentine   thick bone-like tissue that makes up most of a tooth

diarrhoea   when the faeces are loose and watery

digestive system   organs of the body that are used to digest food

dissolve   when a solid or gas merges with a liquid

DNA   substance that genes are made from. DNA carries the genetic information that makes you a unique individual

duodenum   first part of the small intestine

eczema   skin disorder which causes patches of very dry, itchy skin and small red pimples

element   simple substance made up of only one kind of chemical

energy   ability to do work or to make something happen

enzyme   substance that helps a chemical change take place faster without being changed itself

fats   substances in some foods that your body uses to provide energy. Fat is stored by your body in a layer below the skin and helps to keep you warm.

fatty acid   kind of acid found in animal fat and vegetable oils and fats

fibre   in food, the undigested parts of plants

free radicals   chemicals that can cause cancer and heart disease

genetic code   instructions that tell your cells what to do and how to make new cells

haemoglobin   chemical in your red blood cells that carries oxygen

hormones   substances produced by different glands in the body that affect or control particular organs, cells or tissues

infectious   easily spread from one person to another

molecule   smallest part of a substance that can exist and still be that substance

neutralize   to make something neutral, that is, neither acid nor alkaline

nutrients   parts of food that your body needs to get energy, to build and repair cells, and for the cells to function properly. Nutrients include carbohydrates, fats, proteins, vitamins and minerals.

oesophagus   tube through which food travels from the mouth to the stomach

organ   part of the body with a specific function. An organ is made up of different kinds of tissue.

ovaries   parts of a woman's body where eggs are produced. An egg has to join with a male sperm to form a baby.

oxygen   invisible gas that is one of the gases in the air. The body needs oxygen in order to break down sugar to form energy.

pharynx   back of the throat

premature   happening too soon. A premature baby is one that is born before it is due.

proteins   complex chemicals that the body needs to grow and repair cells

puberty age when the body begins to produce sex hormones and becomes able to reproduce sexually

retina nerve cells at the back of the eye that react to light

saliva watery liquid made by glands in your mouth and the inside of your cheeks

soluble able to dissolve in liquid

spina bifida inherited disease that affects the spine

starch carbohydrates stored in plants

stress strain or pressure

stroke when a blood vessel in the brain bursts or is blocked by a clot of blood, damaging part of the brain

tissue part of the body made up of the same kind of cells

thyroid gland gland that effects growth and the production of energy and waste in the body

trace element mineral that is important for health but is only needed in very small quantities.

Resources

Books

Body Needs: Fats, Jillian Powell (Heinemann Library, 2003)

DEFRA Manual of Nutrition, (HMSO, 1995)

Digesting: How we fuel the body, Angela Royston (Franklin Watts, 1998)

Websites

www.daily-vitamins.com/
Website with information about how the body uses all kinds of vitamins and minerals.

www.mckinley.uiuc.edu/Handouts/reducesodiumdiet.html
Tells you more about salt and how to reduce it in your diet.

www.mckinley.uiuc.edu/Handouts/vitaminmineral.html
Tells you about the main vitamins and minerals and which foods contain them.

www.mckinley.uiuc.edu/health-info/nutrit/phytochemicals.htm
Tells you about vitamins and minerals found in plants.

www.NutritionAustralia.org
This is the information service of the Australian Nutrition Foundation.

www.nutrition.org.uk/
Web site of the British Nutrition Foundation which gives information on all aspects of diet, including vitamins and minerals. Click on nutrients to get started.

www.realtime.net/anr/anrrda.html
For information about beta-carotene, antioxidants and other facts about vitamins and minerals.

www3.utsouthwestern.edu/library/consubj/vitamin.htm
Deals with particular issues, such as allergies, and particular vitamins and minerals, such as calcium.

Disclaimer
All the Internet addresses (URLs) given in this book were valid at the time of going to press. However, due to the dynamic nature of the Internet, some addresses may have changed, or sites may have ceased to exist since publication. While the author and publishers regret any inconvenience this may cause readers, no responsibility for any such changes can be accepted by either the author or the publishers.

Index

amino acids 18
anaemia 34, 35, 37
antioxidants 17, 21

babies 29, 30, 31, 35, 40, 41
bacteria 15, 21, 23
balanced diet 28, 32, 38–39
beriberi 33
beta-carotenes 8, 16,
biotin 18,
birth defects 29, 40
blood 18, 21, 26, 27, 30, 34, 35, 37
body fluids 22, 24–5
bone marrow 16, 18
bones and teeth 11, 20, 22, 23, 30, 31, 35, 37

calcium 7, 10, 11, 20, 22–3, 29, 35, 36, 37, 38, 40, 43
cancer 16, 20
carbohydrates 4, 5, 6, 12, 14, 16, 18, 38
cells 4, 5, 16, 17, 18, 24, 26, 37, 38
cholesterol 17
connective tissue 19

deficiency diseases 32–37
digestive system 12–15, 20, 26, 38
DNA 16

energy 4, 5, 16, 18, 26, 38
enzymes 12, 16, 15, 22, 26
eyesight 17, 34

fats 4, 5, 6, 12, 14, 16, 17, 18, 38
fatty acids 15
fibre 38
fluoride 11, 23, 30, 31
folate 16, 18, 34, 40
free radicals 16, 21
fruit and vegetables 6, 8, 9, 11, 17, 19, 38

goitre 37

haemoglobin 18, 26, 27, 37
heart disease 17, 20
high blood pressure 30
hormones 21, 27

iodine 37, 11, 27
iron 7, 10, 11, 15, 19, 26, 27, 34, 37, 40, 43

magnesium 10, 11, 22, 24, 37
meat and fish 11, 38

mercury 31
milk and dairy produce 11, 31, 38
minerals 4, 6, 7, 10–11
    deficiencies 36–37
    digesting 12–15
    functions 22–7
    recommended daily amounts 42

niacin 18, 29, 33
nutrients 4, 6, 14, 16, 24, 32, 38, 40

older people 32, 36, 41
osteoporosis 36, 37

pellagra 33
phosphorus 10, 22, 24, 30
potassium 10, 11, 24, 37
pregnant women 29, 31, 40
proteins 4, 5, 6, 12, 14, 16, 18, 24, 38

riboflavin 18
rickets 35, 36

salt 11, 24, 25, 30, 31, 36, 41
scurvy 6, 34
sodium 10, 11, 24, 43
supplements 28–29, 40
sweat 24, 25, 36, 41

thiamin 8, 18, 33, 43
trace elements 11, 23, 27

vegetarians and vegans 40
vitamins 4, 6, 8–9
    deficiencies 32–35
    digesting 12–15
    fat-soluble vitamins 8, 15, 20, 29, 33, 38
    functions 16–21
    recommended daily amounts 42
    Vitamin A 8, 17, 29, 34, 41
    Vitamin B 8, 9, 14, 15, 18, 29, 33, 34, 38, 40
    Vitamin C 6, 8, 9, 14, 15, 16, 18, 19, 27, 29, 34, 40, 41, 42, 43
    Vitamin D 8, 9, 20, 23, 29, 33, 35, 40, 41
    Vitamin E 8, 16, 20, 21, 29, 35
    Vitamin K 8, 9, 20, 21, 29, 35
    water-soluble vitamins 8, 9, 18, 29

wound healing 6, 19, 21, 27, 35

zinc 10, 15, 27